NATIONAL GEOGRAPHIC GUIDE TO THE
CIVIL WAR
National Battlefield Parks

By A. Wilson Greene
and Gary W. Gallagher

Photography by Sam Abell

PUBLISHED BY
THE NATIONAL GEOGRAPHIC SOCIETY

Gilbert M. Grosvenor
President & Chairman of the Board

Michela A. English
Senior Vice President

William R. Gray
Vice President & Director, Book Division

Margery G. Dunn, Charles Kogod
Assistant Directors, Book Division

Leah Bendavid-Val
Senior Editor, Book Division

PRODUCED BY THE BOOK DIVISION AND
ELLIOTT & CLARK PUBLISHING, INC.

A. Wilson Greene
Gary W. Gallagher
Authors

Sam Abell
Photography

Gibson Parsons Design
Art Direction and Design

Kimberly A. Kostyal
William J. Miller
Researchers

Richard S. Wain
Production Project Manager

Karen Dufort Sligh
Illustrations Assistant

Edwin C. Bearss
Jay Luvaas
Consultants

Manufacturing and Quality Management
George V. White
Director

John T. Dunn
Associate Director

CARTOGRAPHY BY
R. R. DONNELLEY & SONS CO.

(Cover photograph) 40th New York Infantry Monument, Gettysburg.

CONTENTS

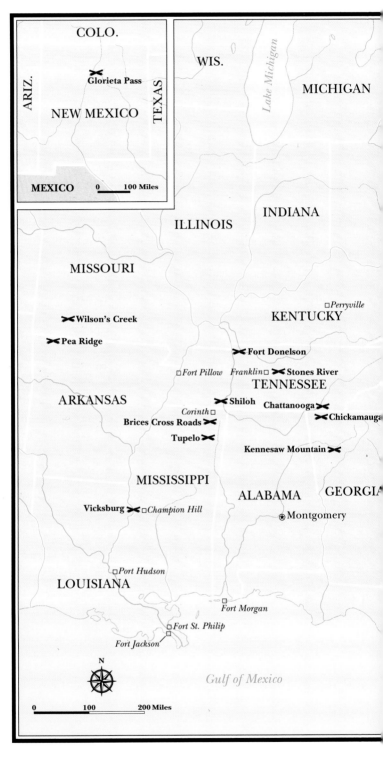

COLO.

ARIZ.

NEW MEXICO

✕ Glorieta Pass

TEXAS

MEXICO   0   100 Miles

WIS.

Lake Michigan

MICHIGAN

INDIANA

ILLINOIS

MISSOURI

✕ Wilson's Creek

✕ Pea Ridge

□ Perryville

KENTUCKY

✕ Fort Donelson

□ Fort Pillow   Franklin □ ✕ Stones River

TENNESSEE

ARKANSAS

Corinth □   ✕ Shiloh   Chattanooga ✕

Brices Cross Roads ✕   ✕ Chickamauga

Tupelo ✕

Kennesaw Mountain ✕

MISSISSIPPI

GEORGIA

ALABAMA

Vicksburg ✕ □ Champion Hill

⊛ Montgomery

□ Port Hudson

LOUISIANA

□ Fort Morgan

□ Fort St. Philip

Fort Jackson □

N

Gulf of Mexico

0   100   200 Miles

4

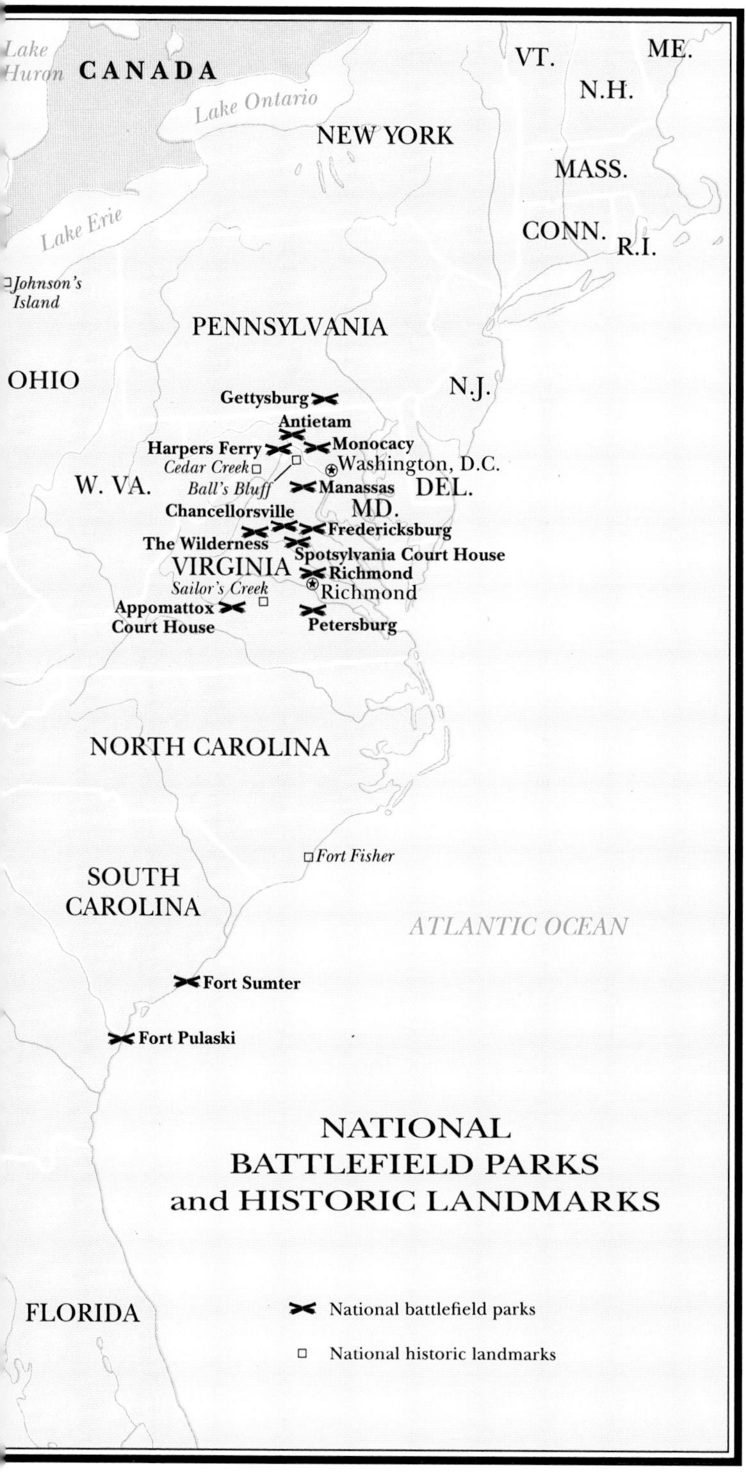

Lake Huron

CANADA

Lake Ontario

VT.

ME.

N.H.

NEW YORK

MASS.

Lake Erie

CONN.

R.I.

□ *Johnson's Island*

PENNSYLVANIA

OHIO

N.J.

Gettysburg ✕

Antietam

Harpers Ferry ✕ ✕ Monocacy

Cedar Creek □ ⊙ Washington, D.C.

W. VA. *Ball's Bluff* ✕ Manassas DEL.

Chancellorsville MD.

The Wilderness ✕ ✕ Fredericksburg

Spotsylvania Court House

VIRGINIA ✕ Richmond

Sailor's Creek ⊛ Richmond

Appomattox ✕ □
Court House ✕
Petersburg

NORTH CAROLINA

□ *Fort Fisher*

SOUTH
CAROLINA

ATLANTIC OCEAN

✕ Fort Sumter

✕ Fort Pulaski

NATIONAL
BATTLEFIELD PARKS
and HISTORIC LANDMARKS

FLORIDA

✕ National battlefield parks

□ National historic landmarks

INTRODUCTION

The Civil War touched thousands of American places. Armies campaigned in more than a dozen states, fighting 10,000 engagements that ranged in scale from gigantic struggles at Gettysburg and Chickamauga to skirmishes and guerrilla raids. More than 620,000 men in service perished during the conflict, a total greater than the number of Americans killed in all other wars combined from colonial times through the midpoint of Vietnam. Scarcely a family in North or South emerged from the war without losing a relative or close friend. Payment of this butcher's bill allowed the United States to resolve two issues that had vexed its society for decades: The presence of slavery would no longer mock the words of the Declaration of Independence, and the Union was confirmed as a true nation rather than a collection of semi-independent states.

The battles that helped shape the outcome of our greatest national trial continue to command our attention. Every year, many thousands of Americans visit fields and woods, forts and even city streets where the Civil War unfolded—a roster of sites too numerous to survey in a traveler's guide. Our handbook, therefore, describes only battlefields and historic landmarks managed by the National Park Service. These holdings cover most of the war's renowned campaigns, but state and local agencies also maintain dozens of important battlegrounds.

Our guide surveys Civil War sites state by state in 16 chapters covering nine Confederate states, six Union states, and the territory of New Mexico. Each chapter features an essay by Gary W. Gallagher, who defines that state's overall role in the war, reviewing political events, contributions of manpower and material goods, and major leaders and military operations. In addition, A. Wilson Greene contributes 23 essays about campaigns and battles in the 11 states where the National Park Service administers Civil War battlegrounds. Greene describes strategic and tactical movements, evaluates the generalship of prominent officers, and assesses the impact of their operations.

The maps complement the narrative, depicting roads, buildings, and natural features as they appeared during the Civil War. We have omitted later additions such as modern highways and National Park Service facilities. We hope that maps and text combined will help you understand the essential elements of each operation.

We should comment on statistics about men in service. Statistics from the Civil War—like those from other modern wars—are imperfect. They reflect inconsistent reports, and not all of these reports have survived. Moreover, the reports distinguish "aggregate present," the total number of men who must be fed and moved, from combat personnel, who fight. Some sources use the first category, some the second. Casualty returns from particular battles changed in successive reports as officers gathered new information. Also, commanders naturally tended to overestimate the enemy's numbers and magnify his losses. Figures for strengths and casualties given in postwar accounts by participants, who frequently wrote to justify their own actions or to criticize those of their foe, should be used with special care. We base our numbers for combat forces engaged and for casualties on the best modern scholarship. In standard military usage, casualties include killed, wounded, missing, and captured.

The photographs that accompany our text convey the beauty of many Civil War sites today. Walking the ground where hundreds of thousands of Americans waged bitter struggles for their respective national goals can be a very moving experience. At few other historic places can one so easily summon ghosts of the past.

Nor do many other sites lend themselves so readily to contem-plation of historic events. Climbing a slope where hundreds died to seize a hilltop, or walking through a simple farmhouse where surgeons worked feverishly on the wounded, we begin to grasp the price that common soldiers paid to renew our nation. Hearing these men's names, seeing their faces in photographs, reading their stories, we meet again a distant generation, already old when our grandparents were young. We begin to understand what these men were like and why they fought. That knowledge is essential to an understanding of the main currents of United States history. If we protect and preserve the battlegrounds of the Civil War, we guarantee that future generations of Americans will also benefit from these links to the past.

MASTER MAP LEGEND

U.S.	C.S.			
▬▬	▬▬	Infantry	————	Road
▪	▪	Cavalry	··········	Trail
⚓	⚓	Artillery	++++	Railroad
▐	▐	Commander's Hq.	—+—+	Unfinished R.R.
⬠	⬠	Fort	–··–··–	State boundary
▲	▲	Camp	––·––·–	Farm boundary
⬭	⬭	Vessel	✕	Battle site
⬅	⬅	Line of march	- - - - -	Battle dividing line
———	———	Fortifications and trenches	〰〰〰	Pontoon bridge
——•——			≈	Bridge
		Open ground	•	Town
		Woodland	▪	Building
		Swamp	⚲	Church
			▭	Dam

ALABAMA

Alabama played a key role in the secession movement and the creation of a Confederate nation in 1861. Led by fire-eater William L. Yancey, secessionist politicians prevailed in a state convention, which voted 61–39 in favor of leaving the Union on January 11, 1861. Moderate sentiment in the hill country of northern Alabama, which also harbored many Unionists, explained the relatively narrow margin by which Alabama became the fourth state to secede.

Montgomery became the Confederacy's first capital when representatives from seven Southern states met there in February 1861 to form a government. They declared themselves a provisional Congress, chose Jefferson Davis as President, and drafted a constitution. After Virginia joined the Confederacy in April, the capital was moved to Richmond.

Of the 526,271 whites living in Alabama in 1860, between 75,000 and 125,00 joined the Confederate army. Union forces enlisted 4,969 blacks, drawn from the state's 435,080 enslaved and 2,850 free blacks, as well as 2,578 Alabama whites. Sixteen Confederate generals, including John Hunt Morgan, named Alabama as their birthplace, as did David Bell Birney and three other Union generals. Estimates of Alabama troops who died during the war range from 25,000 to nearly 70,000, with the true figure closer to the former. Cahaba Prison near Selma held 5,000 Union prisoners between mid-1863 and the end of the war.

The Confederacy relied heavily on Alabama's industrial resources.

During the war, the state's ironworks produced an average of 40,000 tons a year and its munitions plants converted much of that iron into ordnance. Selma became a leading Southern manufacturing center. Agricultural products also flowed from Alabama throughout the Confederacy until late in the war, when the South's transportation network was fractured by territorial losses.

Although Alabama witnessed more than 325 military events, no major land battle took place within its borders. The North gained control of the Tennessee River Valley early in 1862, after which notable Union raids into the state were mounted by Col. Abel

Casemates, Fort Morgan

D. Streight in the spring of 1863, Maj. Gen. Lovell H. Rousseau in the summer of 1864, and Brig. Gen. James H. Wilson in the spring of 1865. Wilson's was the most effective; his forces captured Montgomery and wrecked industrial works at Selma and elsewhere.

Mobile became the South's chief Gulf port after New Orleans and Pensacola fell to the Union in 1862. Defended by Fort Morgan, Fort Gaines, and other substantial fortifications, Mobile Bay remained open until the last year of the war. On August 5, 1864, a fleet under Rear Adm. David G. Farragut passed Forts Morgan and Gaines, defeated the ironclad *Tennessee* and a small Southern fleet in the bay,

and effectively closed the port of Mobile. The city itself capitulated on April 13, 1865. Three weeks later, on May 4, Lt. Gen. Richard Taylor surrendered the remaining Confederate forces in Alabama to Maj. Gen. E. R. S. Canby at Citronelle, some 40 miles north of Mobile.

National Historic Landmark

FORT MORGAN
For information, contact:
51 Highway 180 West
Gulf Shores, AL 36542
(202) 540-7125
Located 22 miles west of Gulf Shores on Ala. 180.

ARKANSAS

D elegates in Arkansas convened twice in the spring of
1861 before they voted to
secede from the Union—a choice
that would disrupt virtually every
aspect of the frontier state's society.
The first convention in March was
evenly divided between secessionists and Unionists. After Fort
Sumter was fired upon, a second
convention on May 6 voted 69–1
to leave the Union. The counties
of the south and east, where the
largest numbers of slaves were
owned, eagerly supported the new
nation, but the north and mountainous northwest displayed little
enthusiasm.

Patterns of military service reflected the state's divided loyalties.
From an 1860 population of
324,143 whites and 111,307 blacks
(all but 192 of whom were slaves),
Arkansas furnished about 60,000
white men to the Confederate
army and 8,289 white and 5,526
black soldiers to the Union army.
Overall, slightly more than two-
thirds of military-age Arkansans
served on one side or the other,
and fully a quarter of them died.
Although no generals were born in
Arkansas, several claimed the state
as their own, including Confederates Patrick Ronayne Cleburne
and Thomas C. Hindman.

With only 38 miles of railroads
and virtually no industry, Arkansas
contributed few manufactured
goods to the Confederate effort.
A primitive transportation network,
which was further disordered as
armies campaigned across the
state, hindered the movement of
agricultural goods. By the middle

of the war Arkansas had ceased to
be a viable part of the Confederacy.

Political events within the state
confirmed this fact. After Federals
under Maj. Gen. Frederick Steele
captured Little Rock on September
10, 1863, Unionists in the northern half of the state moved to
create a loyalist government.
In March 1864 Unionist voters
ratified a new constitution that
abolished slavery. As governor they
chose Isaac Murphy, who had cast
the single vote against secession in
May 1861. A Confederate state
government under Harris Flanagin
continued to function at Washington in southwestern Arkansas until
late in the war.

More than 770 military events

David Muench

■ *Elkhorn Tavern, Pea Ridge*

occurred in Arkansas. The first important battle was at Pea Ridge (or Elkhorn Tavern) on March 7–8, 1862, where Brig. Gen. Samuel R. Curtis solidified Union control over Missouri by defeating Confederates under Maj. Gen. Earl Van Dorn. In mid-July 1862 Curtis captured Helena, an important town on the Mississippi River which the Federals successfully defended against a Confederate army a year later. In late 1862 Maj. Gen. Thomas C. Hindman sought to reclaim northwestern Arkansas for the Confederacy, but his forces were defeated on December 7 in the Battle of Prairie Grove. Arkansas Post, below Helena on the Arkansas River, fell to Union Maj. Gen. John A. McClernand on January 11, 1863, early in Grant's Vicksburg Campaign.

The last significant campaigning in Arkansas took place in conjunction with Maj. Gen. Nathaniel P. Banks's ineffectual Red River Campaign during the spring of 1864. A Union army under Maj. Gen. Frederick Steele marched south from Little Rock, occupying Camden on April 15 and fighting a sharp engagement at Jenkins' Ferry on April 30 before retiring to Little Rock. Military operations ceased in Arkansas when Lt. Gen. E. Kirby Smith surrendered his Trans-Mississippi forces on May 26, 1865.

PEA RIDGE

During the first year of the Civil War, North and South contended more fiercely for control of Missouri than for any other border slave state. But the battle that secured Missouri for the Union occurred at Pea Ridge, in neighboring northwestern Arkansas, on March 7–8, 1862.

The campaign opened in December 1861 when a former Iowa congressman, Brig. Gen. Samuel R. Curtis, took command of the Union army in southwestern Missouri. Curtis had orders to drive the Rebels from the state. In February 1862 he bloodlessly achieved his purpose by marching toward the Confederate stronghold at Springfield. The pro-Southern Missouri State Guard, under former governor Sterling Price, retreated with little fighting into Arkansas's Boston Mountains. On the way they joined another Confederate force led by Benjamin McCulloch.

Price and McCulloch did not get along, so the Confederate government assigned Maj. Gen. Earl Van Dorn, a Mississippi firebrand with solid military credentials, to overall command in the Trans-Mississippi. Van Dorn nurtured ambitious plans. "I must

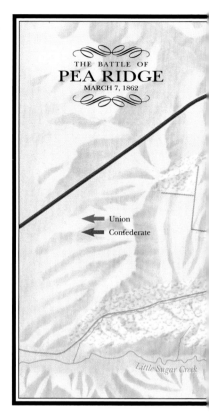

THE BATTLE OF
PEA RIDGE
MARCH 7, 1862

Union
Confederate

Little Sugar Creek

have St. Louis—then huzza!" he wrote his wife. Van Dorn augmented his army with a thousand Native Americans led by 300-pound eccentric Brig. Gen. Albert Pike. Pea Ridge would be one of the few major Civil War battles in

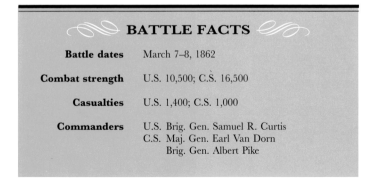

⤜ **BATTLE FACTS** ⤛

Battle dates	March 7–8, 1862
Combat strength	U.S. 10,500; C.S. 16,500
Casualties	U.S. 1,400; C.S. 1,000
Commanders	U.S. Brig. Gen. Samuel R. Curtis C.S. Maj. Gen. Earl Van Dorn Brig. Gen. Albert Pike

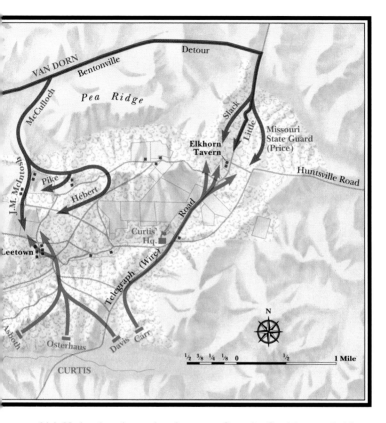

which Native Americans played a large role.

On March 4 Van Dorn steered his 17,000 men north toward Curtis's army, which had trailed Price into Arkansas. When scouts told Curtis of the Confederate approach, he ordered his 11,000 troops to fall back. Just in time, the four Union divisions took up a strong position behind Little Sugar Creek along the Wire Road. Van Dorn's advance arrived on their heels, gobbling up part of the Federal rear guard before it reached the creek. The Confederates had come up with astonishing speed, crossing 55 miles of rough country in two days in a snow-storm.

Opposite Curtis's stronghold, Van Dorn halted and devised a plan. Instead of tackling the Federal entrenchments head-on, Van Dorn decided on an eight-mile flank march that would place his army behind the enemy. Price's Missourians drew the toughest assignment. Using a byway that skirted Pea Ridge's western end, Price would land on the Wire Road north of Little Sugar Creek near Elkhorn Tavern. McCulloch and Pike would secretly move toward the hamlet of Leetown, northwest of the Union position, and attack from there. With Confederates on his flank and rear and across his line of supply and retreat, Curtis could not escape a decisive thrashing.

Leaving campfires burning to deceive the Federals, Van Dorn launched his exhausted men on their long trek on the night of March 6–7. They had difficulty fording icy Little Sugar Creek and encountered obstructions on the narrow roads. When the sun rose, they were not yet in position.

Curtis reacted to the Confederate maneuver by sending a division under Col. Eugene A. Carr to Elkhorn Tavern. There, Price and Carr slugged it out through the day, the outnumbered Federals slowly giving ground until a fresh division relieved them near nightfall.

Near Leetown, McCulloch's command drove Union Col. Peter Osterhaus's troops from the battlefield. Curtis reinforced Osterhaus

with a division led by an Indianan ironically named Jefferson C. Davis, and Davis stabilized the situation. Pike's Native Americans grew demoralized by Union artillery fire; McCulloch's men lost heart when their leader was killed by an Illinois sharpshooter. Late in the day a Federal counterattack regained the lost ground and sent the Confederates fleeing. After dark Pike led the remnants of McCulloch's command to the Wire Road where they joined Van Dorn and Price.

Van Dorn's plan had failed. His men were tired, hungry, and low on ammunition, and his supply wagons had been left behind. Hoping that his opponents were in equally sorry condition, Van Dorn remained on the battlefield and

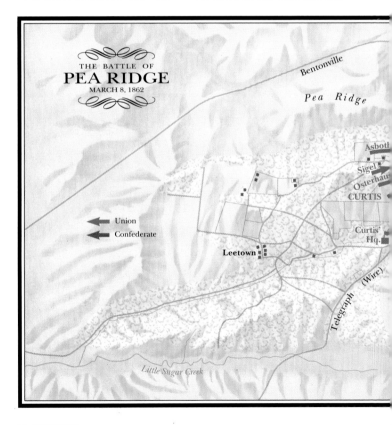

THE BATTLE OF
PEA RIDGE
MARCH 8, 1862

Bentonville

Pea Ridge

Asboth

Sigel

Osterhaus

CURTIS

Curtis' Hq.

Leetown

Telegraph (Wire)

Union
Confederate

Little Sugar Creek

challenged Curtis to renew the attack on March 8.

This bluff almost worked. At a council of war held during the night, nearly all of Curtis's subordinates advised retreat. Curtis rejected their advice and ordered an attack in the morning.

The Union artillery opened the second day's fighting, systematically knocking out Confederate batteries. The Yankees then charged, Van Dorn's resistance crumbled, and the Confederates fled.

In his official report, Van Dorn asserted that "I was not defeated, but only foiled in my intentions." But in fact, the Richmond authorities ordered Van Dorn's army to abandon Arkansas after Pea Ridge and help defend Mississippi. The Confederates would not make another organized attempt to control Missouri until September 1864.

PARK INFORMATION

HEADQUARTERS: Pea Ridge National Military Park, Pea Ridge, AR 72751. Telephone: (501) 451-8122.

DIRECTIONS: From Rogers, Arkansas, proceed 10 miles northeast on US 62 to park entrance. From Fayetteville, take US 71 20 miles north to Bentonville, and follow Ark. 72 east to where it meets US 62. Continue east on 62 to park.

SCHEDULE: Open daily from 8 a.m. to 5 p.m. Closed Thanksgiving, Christmas, and New Year's Day.

ENTRANCE FEE: Ages 17–61, $1.00.

TOURS: From Visitor Center parking area, 7-mile, self-guided auto tour leads through 4,300-acre park. Eleven wayside markers provide information at significant sites. Hiking and riding trails available.

POINT OF INTEREST: **Elkhorn Tavern** Original structure was twice center of fighting. Rebuilt. Marker 8.

NEARBY HISTORIC INNS: ■ Crescent Hotel (1886), Eureka Springs; (501) 253-9766 or (800) 643-4972. ■ Elmwood House (1886), Eureka Springs; (501) 253-7227. ■ Grand Central Hotel (1883), Eureka Springs; (501) 253-6756 or (800) 643-4972. ■ Heart of the Hills (1883), Eureka Springs; (501) 253-7468. ■ The Johnson House (1882), Johnson; (501) 756-1095. ■ Ridgeway House (1908), Eureka Springs; (501) 253-6618.

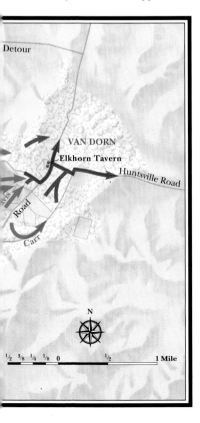

GEORGIA

T he largest, wealthiest, and most populous state of the Deep South, Georgia left the Union after its state convention voted 208–89 for secession on January 19, 1861. Georgians such as Howell Cobb, T. R. R. Cobb, Robert Toombs, and Alexander H. Stephens (who became vice president of the Confederacy) played key roles in writing a new constitution and setting up the provisional Confederate government in Montgomery, Alabama.

At home, Governor Joseph E. Brown quickly began to mobilize Georgia's military resources. Brown opposed conscription, impressment, and other measures decreed by the Confederate government, and has been criticized for placing Georgia's needs above those of the Confederacy. In fact, the state he governed made ample contributions to the Southern war effort. With a white population in 1860 of 591,550, Georgia sent more than 100,000 soldiers to Confederate armies and enrolled thousands of others in the state militia. Georgia claimed more than 50 general officers in Confederate service, among them James Longstreet, W. J. Hardee, John B. Gordon, and E. P. Alexander.

Georgians in Union armies included an undetermined number of whites and 3,486 blacks, drawn

from the state's 462,198 slaves and 3,538 free blacks. Union generals Montgomery Meigs and John Charles Frémont gave the state as their birthplace. Nearly 13,000 Union soldiers died at Andersonville, the largest and most infamous prison camp of the war.

Fourteen hundred miles of railroads and numerous manufacturing establishments made Georgia a center of production and transportation for the Confederacy. Atlanta became a pivotal supply hub, while Augusta's powder works, the largest in the South, produced 2,750,000 pounds of that critical material. Other important facilities included a government arsenal at Macon and an arsenal and shoe factories at Columbus. On the agricultural side, Georgia's farms sent food and fodder to Southern armies throughout the conflict.

Nearly 550 military events disrupted life in Georgia. Two famous episodes occurred in rapid succession in April 1862. On the 11th, Federals under Capt. Quincy A. Gillmore captured Fort Pulaski and effectively closed the port of Savannah; one day later James J. Andrews and a small band of Northern raiders seized a locomotive named the *General* and led Southern pursuers on the "Great Locomotive Chase" up the Western & Atlantic Railroad between Big Shanty (modern Kennesaw) and Chattanooga, Tennessee.

The interior of Georgia remained largely untouched until Sherman's famous campaigns of 1864. Marching from Chattanooga in May, Sherman confronted first Joseph E. Johnston and then John Bell Hood, suffering a temporary setback at Kennesaw Mountain on June 27 before capturing Atlanta on September 2. After ten weeks in Atlanta, Sherman set out on his "march to the sea," a deliberate effort to demoralize the Confederacy. As they advanced along a 60-mile-wide front, his troops burned property, tore up railroads, and lived off the land. They met little resistance and reached Savannah in a month, taking possession of the city on December 21, 1864. Sherman's army moved on to South Carolina in late January 1865. Its departure ended Georgia's active part in the conflict.

◀ *Kelly House, Chickamauga*

CHICKAMAUGA

The Cherokees called it Chickamauga—River of Death. In 1863 events near this sluggish stream in north Georgia would give new meaning to its ominous name. The Battle of Chickamauga was the bloodiest two-day battle of the Civil War, claiming nearly 35,000 casualties.

In the summer of 1863 Union victories at Gettysburg and Vicksburg overshadowed a less spectacular but no less critical success in Tennessee. Without fighting any battles, Maj. Gen. William S. Rosecrans's Army of the Cumberland maneuvered Gen. Braxton Bragg's Army of Tennessee out of the state's interior. Bragg withdrew to the southeast and deployed his forces around Chattanooga, a vital rail and manufacturing center. Here Rosecrans again outwitted Bragg. Instead of approaching from the northeast as expected, the Federals went southwest and threatened to cut off the Confederates from their supply base at Atlanta. On September 8 Bragg abandoned Chattanooga, again without a fight, and moved 26 miles south to LaFayette, Georgia.

Now it was Rosecrans's turn to be fooled. Thinking that the Rebels were in headlong retreat, the Union commander dangerously divided his three corps of 58,000 men along a 40-mile front and pursued Bragg eastward

BATTLE FACTS

Battle dates	September 19–20, 1863
Combat strength	U.S. 58,000; C.S. 66,000
Casualties	U.S. 16,000; C.S. 18,500
Commanders	U.S. Maj. Gen. William S. Rosecrans C.S. Gen. Braxton Bragg

through rugged mountains. Bragg encouraged Rosecrans's delusion; he strewed the Federals' path with well-rehearsed Rebel deserters who told tales of desperate times in the Army of Tennessee. In fact, Bragg hoped to pounce on isolated fragments of the enemy as they emerged from the mountains.

Bragg's plan might have worked, but on September 10th and again on the 12th, his subordinates failed to execute their orders. Awakening to his vulnerable position, Rosecrans hastily concentrated his three corps west of Chickamauga Creek near Lee & Gordon's Mills on the road from Chattanooga to LaFayette.

Bragg sulked for a few days, but his spirits revived with the news that reinforcements were approaching from Virginia. Led by Lt. Gen. James Longstreet, this corps tipped the numerical scales in Bragg's favor and encouraged him to renew the offensive.

The Confederate plan was simple. Bragg would march north on the east side of Chickamauga Creek, cross the stream beyond the Federal left flank, and separate Rosecrans from his supply line to Chattanooga. The outnumbered Yankees would then be forced either to fight or retreat through the mountains, where pursuing Confederates could cut them to ribbons.

Bragg intended to launch his plan on September 18, but poor roads, slow-moving Confederates,

◄ *Florida State Monument, Chickamauga*

CHICKAMAUGA 19

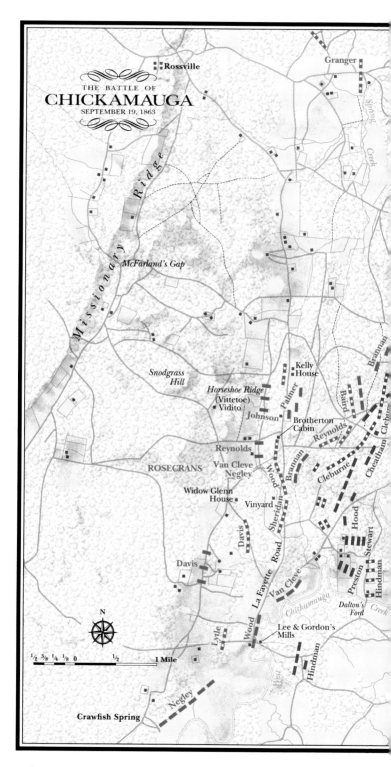

THE BATTLE OF
CHICKAMAUGA
SEPTEMBER 19, 1863

Rossville

Granger

Missionary Ridge

McFarland's Gap

Snodgrass Hill

Kelly House

Palmer

Baird

Horseshoe Ridge
(Vittetoe)
Vidito

Johnson

Brotherton Cabin

Reynolds

Cleburne

Brannan

Reynolds

Van Cleve
Negley

ROSECRANS

Wood

Cleburne

Cheatham

Widow Glenn House

Vinyard

Sheridan

Hood

Davis

La Fayette Road

Preston
Stewart

Hindman

Davis

Wood

Van Cleve

Chickamauga

Dalton's Ford

Creek

N

Lytle

Wood

Lee & Gordon's Mills

1/2 3/8 1/4 1/8 0   1/2   1 Mile

Hindman

Negley

Crawfish Spring

West

Spring Creek

Brannan

and stubborn Union cavalry conspired to delay the creek crossing. Reacting to the Confederate initiative, Rosecrans spent the night shifting his army north. He placed his best corps commander, Maj. Gen. George H. Thomas, on the critical left flank. As dawn broke on September 19 in the thick woods west of Chickamauga Creek, the Federals actually outflanked their opponents at the north end of a four-mile line.

An Alabama soldier described the fighting on the 19th as "one solid, unbroken wave of awe-inspiring sound…as if all the fires of earth and hell had been turned loose in one mighty effort to destroy each other." Bragg, still hoping to slice between Rosecrans and Chattanooga, ordered a sequence of attacks from north to south designed to push the bluecoats into a mountain hollow known as McLemore's Cove. In wave after wave, his brigades punished the Union line but failed to break it. Rosecrans rushed reinforcements to Thomas throughout the day. When the firing died away after dark, the Federals still held firm.

That night, while Rosecrans strengthened his position with logs and earth, Longstreet reported to Confederate headquarters. Bragg, whose relations with subordinates were rarely congenial, had inexplicably decided to restructure his command in the middle of the night and the battle. He assigned Longstreet to the left wing and Lt. Gen. Leonidas Polk, an Episcopal bishop with modest military talent, to the right. Bragg called for a renewal of combat at dawn, relying once again on a sequence of attacks from north to south.

One of Polk's corps, under Lt. Gen. D. H. Hill, was to open the

battle on the 20th. But Bragg's orders did not reach Hill until after daybreak, and even then the petulant North Carolinian readied his men with undue deliberation. Obviously the Army of Tennessee had problems at the highest levels of command.

Around 9:30 a.m., some four hours behind schedule, Polk's divisions finally attacked Thomas. The rank and file hurled themselves at the Union barricades with a fury that belied their uninspired leadership. The Federals met the onslaughts bravely, as Thomas repeatedly called on Rosecrans to bolster his beleaguered position with fresh troops from the Union center and right.

The turning point at Chickamauga resulted from an error—no surprise in a battle marked by shaky generalship. A Union officer, failing to see a Northern division in the thick forest, told Rosecrans that a gap existed in his line. Without verifying this startling news, Rosecrans ordered one of his divisions to pull out of position and plug the alleged gap. Naturally, the removal

of these troops created a real gap. As luck would have it, Longstreet's scheduled assault struck this precise point moments after the Union withdrawal.

Sixteen thousand Confederates streamed through the hole, routing the better part of four Union divisions and capturing three dozen cannon. Rosecrans and two of his corps commanders dashed with their men to the safety of Chattanooga. Not since the first battle of Manassas had a Union army fled the field in such disorder.

But some Union troops did not run. Thomas's command—about half the army—reshaped the line to face south as well as east and hunkered down around an elevated farmstead called Snodgrass Hill. Thomas told his officers, "This hill must be held," and his subordinates responded, "We will hold it or die here."

Longstreet regrouped his victorious Rebels, and in midafternoon he renewed the offensive against Thomas's new line. The Federals repulsed every attack, aided by two fresh brigades under Maj. Gen. Gordon Granger. On his own authority Granger had advanced from a reserve position north of the battlefield, bringing much-needed ammunition.

Polk's wing did not pressure Thomas from the east until later in the afternoon. When both Confederate wings began to strike together, Thomas knew his position was hopeless. The Union withdrawal started shortly before sunset, and the Federals fought desperately against the final Confederate thrusts. At last Thomas guided his survivors through McFarland's Gap in Missionary Ridge, and the Battle of Chickamauga concluded.

The Army of Tennessee had won its greatest victory, but Bragg did not seem to realize it. Ignoring the advice of Longstreet, Nathan Bedford Forrest, and others, Bragg refused to pursue the defeated enemy. Rosecrans fortified Chattanooga, ending whatever chance there might have been to destroy his army. Now Bragg would have to besiege the city, a strategy that would lead in two months to a disastrous new series of battles and the end of his career with the Army of Tennessee.

PARK INFORMATION

HEADQUARTERS: Chickamauga and Chattanooga National Military Park, P. O. Box 2128, Fort Oglethorpe, GA 30742. Telephone: (706) 866-9241.

DIRECTIONS: From I-24, exit south onto Rossville Blvd. (US 27). From I-75, exit west at Battlefield Parkway (Ga. 2) to Fort Oglethorpe and turn left onto US 27.

SCHEDULE: Grounds open daily during daylight hours. Visitor centers at Chickamauga Battlefield and Point Park open from 8 a.m. to 4:45 p.m. and from Memorial Day to Labor Day until 5:45 p.m. Closed Christmas. Historic Cravens House open during summer season from 9 a.m. to 5 p.m. Monday through Saturday; from 1 to 5 p.m. Sunday.

ENTRANCE FEE: None

TOURS: Park includes more than 8,000 acres in southeast Tennessee and northwest Georgia. Chickamauga Battlefield includes 7-mile, self-guided auto tour with wayside markers and hiking trails. Audiotapes to accompany tour can be rented at Chickamauga Visitor Center bookstore. Organized tours scheduled during summer.

POINTS OF INTEREST: ■ **Chickamauga Battlefield Visitor Center** Begin tour here. Features book store, exhibit rooms, Civil War time line, Fuller Collection of American Military Arms, and multimedia presentation (fee charged for theater). ■ **Point Park Visitor Center** Commands scenic view of Tennessee River below Lookout Mountain. Offers small bookstore, exhibit on signaling, and large painting of battle for Chattanooga. Audio program discusses painting. ■ **Cravens House** Served as headquarters for Confederate officers and was center of intense fighting on November 24, 1863. Cravens rebuilt on site after war; postwar house restored and open to public for small fee. ■ **Ochs Museum and Overlook** Exhibits focus on battle for Chattanooga. Located on Lookout Mountain near Point Park Visitor Center.

NEARBY HISTORIC INNS: Bed and Breakfast Hospitality, P. O. Box 110227, Nashville, TN 37222; (615) 331-5244 or (800) 458-2421. Statewide reservation service for historic inns.

FORT PULASKI

American military planners learned a valuable lesson from the War of 1812: The nation's ports presented easy targets for enemy navies. In the ensuing decades, the government built a system of fortifications—including Charleston's Fort Sumter—at key points on the Atlantic, Gulf, and Pacific Coasts.

Savannah's seaward bastion was Fort Pulaski, 15 miles to the east on Cockspur Island at the mouth of the Savannah River. The army named the fort for Count Casimir Pulaski, a Polish hero of the American Revolution who was mortally wounded at Savannah in 1779. When construction began in 1829, one of the engineers was 2nd Lt. Robert E. Lee, fresh from graduation at West Point. Eighteen years, 25 million bricks, and one million dollars later, Fort Pulaski secured Georgia's port city from naval or amphibious assault.

Georgia troops effortlessly seized Fort Pulaski from two Federal caretakers on January 3, 1861. The fort had been poorly maintained, and its new occupants quickly returned it to a defensible condition. Under the direction of 25-year-old Col. Charles Olmstead, the Confederates mounted 48 cannon on the parapet and in the brick casemates. Gen. Robert E. Lee returned to examine the fort and pronounced it impervious to artillery fire.

Quincy A. Gillmore of the U.S. Engineers thought otherwise. In November 1861 Union troops had established a base at nearby Hilton Head Island, South Carolina. From there, Gillmore secretly installed batteries on Tybee Island, a mile from Fort Pulaski. His arsenal included recently developed large-caliber rifled cannon, a more powerful, accurate weapon than the artillery known to Fort Pulaski's designers in 1829.

Meanwhile, other Federal forces severed the fort from its Savannah supply base. The garrison had enough food to hold out for six months, but Union commanders were unwilling to conduct a long siege. Once Gillmore's artillery was in place, the Federals demanded Pulaski's immediate capitulation. "I am here to defend the fort, not to surrender it," replied Olmstead early on April 10, 1862. Minutes later, at 8:10 a.m., Gillmore opened fire.

The bombardment lasted 30 hours, and in that time 5,275 shot and shell hurtled toward the fort. Olmstead had anticipated a shell-

❧ BATTLE FACTS ❧

Battle dates	April 10–11, 1862
Combat strength	U.S. 1,000; C.S. 385
Casualties	U.S. 1; C.S. 1 killed, 384 captured
Commanders	U.S. Maj. Gen. David Hunter Acting Brig. Gen. Quincy A. Gillmore C.S. Col. Charles H. Olmstead

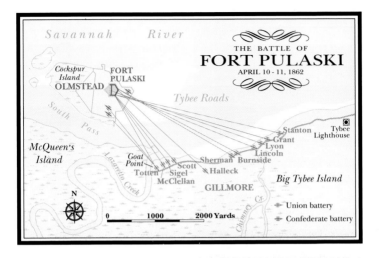

Savannah River

THE BATTLE OF
FORT PULASKI
APRIL 10 - 11, 1862

Cockspur Island
FORT PULASKI
OLMSTEAD

Tybee Roads

South Pass

McQueen's Island

Lazaretto Creek

Goat Point
Totten
Scott
Sigel
McClellan

Sherman
Halleck
GILLMORE

Stanton
Grant
Lyon
Lincoln
Burnside

Tybee Lighthouse

Big Tybee Island

Chimney Cr.

N

0   1000   2000 Yards

⚏ Union battery
⚏ Confederate battery

ing that heavy, but not the results. The Union's rifled cannon peeled away Fort Pulaski's seven-foot-six-inch-thick masonry walls. When the walls had been breached, the fort's powder magazines became vulnerable. Rather than risk a catastrophic explosion, Olmstead reluctantly raised a white flag at 2 p.m. on April 11.

The entire garrison of 385 men, less one killed and a few wounded, boarded ships for Union prisons. With the Federals controlling the mouth of the river, blockade-running all but ceased in Savannah.

Moreover, the rapid reduction of Fort Pulaski marked the demise of masonry fortifications. The Union commander in the south Atlantic, David Hunter, reported: "The result of this bombardment must cause…a change in the construction of fortifications as radical as that foreshadowed in naval architecture by the conflict between the Monitor and the Merrimac. No works of stone or brick can resist the impact of rifled artillery of heavy caliber."

PARK INFORMATION

HEADQUARTERS: Fort Pulaski National Monument, P. O. Box 30757, Savannah, GA 31410. Telephone: (912) 786-5787.

DIRECTIONS: From Savannah take US 80 east for 14 miles to park entrance.

SCHEDULE: Open daily from 8:30 a.m. to 5:15 p.m. and from Memorial Day to Labor Day until 6:45 p.m. Closed Christmas.

ENTRANCE FEE: Ages 17–61, $1.00. Educational groups free.

TOURS: Self-guided walking tour features audio stations with taped messages. From hiking trails outside fort, visitors can see variety of plant and animal life on Cockspur Island.

NEARBY HISTORIC INNS: R.S.V.P. Georgia and Savannah Bed & Breakfast Reservation Service, 417 E. Charlton St., Savannah, GA 31401; (912) 232-7787 or (800) 729-7787. Statewide reservation service for historic inns.

KENNESAW MOUNTAIN

"Atlanta was too important a place in the hands of the enemy to be left undisturbed, with its magazines, stores, arsenal, workshops, foundries, and more especially its railroads, which converged there from the four great cardinal points." So wrote Maj. Gen. William T. Sherman, U.S.A., about the goal of his ambitious campaign in the spring of 1864. With much of east Tennessee in Federal hands, Sherman was able to marshal three separate armies, totaling more than 100,000 men. On May 4 they set out from the northwest corner of Georgia, a hundred miles from Atlanta. Sherman's route lay along the Western & Atlantic Railroad—a critical link to his Nashville supply base as he advanced deep into hostile territory.

Mountains, rivers, and the 65,000 men of Gen. Joseph E. Johnston's Army of Tennessee blocked his path. Unlike Lee and Grant, who fought a series of enormous, costly pitched battles that year, Sherman and Johnston relied on maneuver in the contest for Atlanta. Johnston sought to halt Sherman by building elaborate entrenchments along strong natural positions. Each time, however, the Northerners outflanked him to the south. Johnston then packed up his army and redeployed at the next defensible spot, only to watch the pattern be repeated. By mid-June, Sherman had pushed Johnston to a point 30 miles northwest of Atlanta without having engaged in a full-scale battle.

On June 18 Johnston again fell back, taking a position north and west of Marietta, an important

BATTLE FACTS

Battle date	June 27, 1864
Combat strength	U.S. 110,000; C.S. 65,000
Casualties	U.S. 3,000; C.S. 1,000
Commanders	U.S. Maj. Gen. William T. Sherman C.S. Gen. Joseph E. Johnston

town along the rail line. He centered his eight-mile line on Kennesaw Mountain, described by an Illinois soldier as "about 700 feet high…entirely separated from all mountain ranges, and swell[ing] up like a great bulb from the plain."

Sherman resorted to his time-tested strategy of outflanking the Kennesaw barrier, but on June 22 Confederate Lt. Gen. John B.

Hood blunted the Northern move with an attack at Kolb's Farm. Heavy rains made marching difficult; Sherman decided to force the issue with the campaign's first frontal assault. His target was the Rebel right on Kennesaw Mountain, where he guessed that Johnston would least expect to be tested.

Sherman planned the battle with his customary precision. At 8 a.m. on June 27, Union troops would strike at two points. Some 5,500 men were to follow Burnt Hickory Road toward a spur of Kennesaw now known as Pigeon Hill. A larger force, 8,000 strong, would attack a salient farther south in the Confederate line near the Dallas Road. An artillery bombardment would precede the assaults, and reserves stood by to exploit a breakthrough. To confuse Johnston, Sherman ordered diversions against both Confederate flanks.

June 27 dawned with a promise of the heat that would send the mercury soaring close to 100°F. The smaller Union force attacked on schedule, but met immediate resistance. After two hours they had done all they could, suffering

◀ *Kennesaw Mountain*

850 casualties and gaining only meaningless ground.

Sherman's main effort met a similar fate. Veteran Confederate troops under Maj. Gens. Patrick R. Cleburne and Benjamin Franklin Cheatham waited behind strongly fortified lines at the top of a slope and watched their blue-clad opponents wade through a creek, struggle in tangled under-growth, and cross an open field toward the Southern position. The terrain broke up the Union forma-

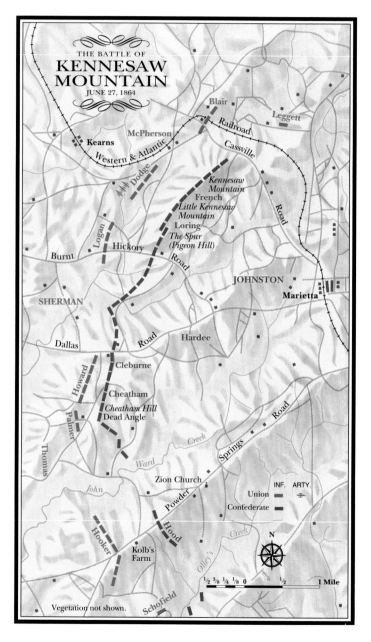

THE BATTLE OF
KENNESAW MOUNTAIN
JUNE 27, 1864

Blair

Leggett

Kearns

McPherson

Railroad

Cassville

Western & Atlantic

Dodge

Kennesaw Mountain

French

Little Kennesaw Mountain

Loring

The Spur (Pigeon Hill)

Road

Logan

Hickory

Burnt

Road

JOHNSTON

Marietta

SHERMAN

Road

Hardee

Dallas

Howard

Cleburne

Cheatham

Palmer

Cheatham Hill
Dead Angle

Thomas

Ward

Creek

Springs

Road

John

Zion Church

INF. ARTY.

Union

Powder

Confederate

Hooker

Hood

Creek

N

Kolb's Farm

Olley's

½ ⅜ ¼ ⅛ 0   ½   1 Mile

Vegetation not shown.

Schofield

tions before they came under serious fire. Nevertheless, they attempted to rush the Rebels' earth embankments, where they met an overwhelming volley of bullets and cannonballs. "The enemy came within five feet of our breastworks and the slaughter was terrific as our troops literally mowed them down," remembered one Confederate. Hand-to-hand fighting ensued at a point in the line called the Dead Angle.

In the end, Union valor proved no match for Confederate determination. The Northerners who survived the attack could not return to their lines without being butchered. Rather than retreat, they dug in 30 yards from the Rebel earthworks. Some of these troops would remain there for six days.

The fighting petered out by noon. When Sherman suggested renewing the attacks, one of his commanders told him, "One or two more such assaults would use up this army." The Battle of Kennesaw Mountain was over.

Of the estimated 16,000 Union soldiers who fought, some 3,000 were killed or wounded. Total Confederate casualties numbered only 1,000. Ironically, Sherman's diversionary movement to the south succeeded in outflanking Johnston's line. On the night of July 2 the Army of Tennessee again withdrew and assumed a new position closer to Atlanta.

Johnston retreated twice more, reaching the outskirts of the city before the Confederate government removed him from command. His successor, Gen. John B. Hood, suffered a series of grievous defeats as he attempted to drive Sherman away, and on September 2, Sherman's men raised the United States flag over Atlanta.

PARK INFORMATION

HEADQUARTERS: Kennesaw Mountain National Battlefield Park, P. O. Box 1610, Marietta, GA 30061. Telephone: (404) 427-4686.

DIRECTIONS: From Atlanta, take I-75 north for 20 miles to exit 116 and follow signs.

SCHEDULE: Open daily from 8:30 a.m. to 5 p.m. Closed Christmas and New Year's Day.

ENTRANCE FEE: None

TOURS: Self-guided auto tour of major sites. Each tour stop provides parking and wayside exhibits. Short interpretive trails located on mountaintop and at Cheatham Hill. Longer hiking trails from 2 to 16 miles round trip. Visitor Center and park headquarters provide general information.

POINTS OF INTEREST:
■ **Kennesaw Mountain** Observation point near summit offers panoramic view of terrain where armies fought. Exhibits and gun emplacements along short trail.
■ **Cheatham Hill** Remains of trenches that formed infamous Dead Angle where Union soldiers fell before Confederate earthworks. Marker 3. ■ **Kolb's Farm** General Hooker used this 1836 log house as headquarters. Restored but not open to public. Marker 4.

NEARBY HISTORIC INNS:
■ The Marlow House (1886), Marietta; (404) 426-1887.
■ The Stanley House (1895), Marietta; (404) 426-1881.

KENTUCKY

No state suffered greater anguish during the secession crisis than Kentucky. Birthplace of both Abraham Lincoln and Jefferson Davis, the state embraced a tradition of compromise on slavery issues personified by its great senator Henry Clay. In 1860 Kentuckians gave Unionist presidential candidate John Bell a majority, and in 1861 the pro-Southern governor, Beriah Magoffin, refused to advocate secession even after the firing on Fort Sumter. He also declined to supply Kentuckians when Presidents Lincoln and Davis issued calls for troops. In May 1861 the state proclaimed its neutrality and announced that neither Union nor Confederate soldiers should set foot in Kentucky.

Kentucky's effort to remain aloof ended on September 3, 1861, when Confederate Maj. Gen. Leonidas Polk occupied Columbus, a strongpoint on the Mississippi River. The pro-Union legislature condemned Polk's action and asked that Federal troops evict the Confederates. A small force under Brig. Gen. Ulysses S. Grant moved immediately to Paducah, and Northern soldiers soon entered the state in large numbers. Southern sympathizers subsequently held a convention and passed an ordinance of secession. Although the Confederate flag contained a star for Kentucky, the state never wavered seriously in its allegiance to the Union.

Kentucky's decision to remain loyal deprived the Confederacy of crucial logistical support. A rich source of horses and mules as well as food, fodder, and leather, the state engaged in a brisk trade with Confederates in Tennessee until Polk occupied Columbus. Kentucky's adherence to the North also shifted the military frontier from the Ohio River south to the Tennessee border, affording the North excellent lines of advance along the Tennessee and Cumberland Rivers and the Louisville & Nashville Railroad.

Divided sentiments showed as Kentucky's citizens entered military service. In 1860 the state was home to 919,484 whites and 236,167 blacks (10,684 of them free). Union armies enlisted 51,743 whites and 23,703 blacks, and roughly 35,000 whites joined the Confederate ranks. Kentuckians who died in uniform included 10,774 Federals and an undetermined number of Confederates.

▶ *Confederate Cemetery, Perryville*

Among 78 general officers born in the state were Confederates John Bell Hood, John C. Breckinridge, and Simon Bolivar Buckner and Federals John Pope and E. R. S. Canby.

More than 450 military actions took place in Kentucky, many of them related to guerrilla warfare that grew increasingly bitter as the war progressed. Striking from Tennessee, Confederate cavalry-man John Hunt Morgan won considerable renown for his daring forays into the state between 1862 and 1864.

Gen. Braxton Bragg commanded the South's most important campaign in Kentucky when he marched into the Bluegrass region in the fall of 1862, hoping to rally Kentuckians to the Confederate cause. His advance coincided with other Southern counteroffensives, including Lee's Maryland Campaign, and involved coordinating his movements with another column under Maj. Gen. E. Kirby Smith. Engagements at Richmond and Munfordville preceded a climactic battle at Perryville on October 7–8, where Bragg's forces fought a Union army under Maj. Gen. Don Carlos Buell. Short of supplies and disappointed by Kentucky's lukewarm response to his presence, Bragg retreated after Perryville. His withdrawal largely extinguished Southern hopes of luring Kentucky into the Confederacy.

National Historic Landmark

■ PERRYVILLE
For information, contact:
Box 296, 1825 Mackville Rd.
Perryville, KY 40468
(606) 332-8631
Located 2 miles north of
Perryville off US 150.

LOUISIANA

F ew Confederate states experienced internal dislocation on the scale endured by Louisiana. In the presidential race of 1860 a majority of the state's voters supported moderate candidates John Bell and Stephen A. Douglas, but Lincoln's election prompted a rapid move toward secession. Governor Thomas A. Moore took control of a number of federal installations, and on January 26, 1861, a state convention voted 113–17 to secede.

The census of 1860 counted 357,456 whites, 331,726 slaves, and 18,647 free blacks in Louisiana. Fifty-six thousand whites joined the Confederate army and 10,000 served in home-guard units, while 5,224 took the Union side, which also enrolled 24,052 blacks. Confederate dead have been estimated at between 6,500

and 15,000, while 945 whites and approximately 5,000 blacks perished in Federal service. P. G. T. Beauregard was the most famous of the seven Confederate generals born in the state. Judah P. Benjamin, a gifted member of Jefferson Davis's cabinet, and diplomat John Slidell were among other prominent Louisianians who served the Confederacy.

The scene of more than 550 military actions, Louisiana lost no significant territory to the Union until the spring of 1862. On April 18–24 a Union squadron under Capt. David G. Farragut bombarded and then ran past Fort Jackson and Fort St. Philip, a pair of masonry structures that had been built just above the mouth of the Mississippi River to protect New Orleans. Farragut's squadron reached New Orleans on April 25 and forced its surrender. The fall of the Crescent City cost the

▼ *Fort Jackson*

Confederacy its largest urban center and seaport, its second largest manufacturing center, and one of its key points for collecting and distributing military supplies. Moreover, the Federals gained an excellent base from which to mount operations up the Mississippi and along the Gulf coast.

During 1862 and 1863 Federal forces penetrated Louisiana's interior, gaining control over much of the state from Alexandria southward. An army under Maj. Gen. Nathaniel P. Banks completed the Union conquest of the Mississippi River on July 8, 1863, when it captured Port Hudson, a stronghold on the river about 25 miles above Baton Rouge. The following spring Banks advanced up the Red River toward Shreveport in the last large military campaign waged in Louisiana. Moving slowly with a combined land and naval force, Banks was turned back by

Confederates under Maj. Gen Richard Taylor at the Battles of Mansfield (or Sabine Crossroads) and Pleasant Hill on April 8–9, 1864.

Louisiana operated under dual governments for much of the war. After Federals captured Baton Rouge, Governor Moore and his successor, Henry W. Allen, operated from Opelousas and later Shreveport. The seat of Federal government was New Orleans. In 1864 voters in areas controlled by the Federals elected Unionist Michael Hahn as their governor, and a constitutional convention held in occupied Louisiana abolished slavery. The war in Louisiana came to a close on May 26, 1865, when the Trans-Mississippi forces of Gen. E. Kirby Smith were surrendered to Maj. Gen. E. R. S. Canby in New Orleans.

National Historic Landmarks

■ FORT JACKSON
For information, contact:
P. O. Box 7043
Buras, LA 70041
(504) 657-7083
Located about 6 miles south of Buras on La. 23.

■ FORT ST. PHILIP
For information, contact:
P. O. Box 7043
Buras, LA 70041
(504) 657-7083
Closed to public.

■ PORT HUDSON
For information, contact:
756 W. Plains—Port Hudson Rd.
Zachary, LA 70791
(504) 654-3775
Located 17 miles north of Baton Rouge on US 61.

MARYLAND

Maryland confronted the crisis of 1860–61 as a deeply divided state. The northern and western areas harbored strong Unionist sentiment, while the eastern and southern counties viewed secession more favorably. But the Union could not afford to let Maryland go; its defection would leave Washington, D. C., isolated in hostile territory.

Several inflammatory events, including a riot in Baltimore on April 19, 1861, when a pro-Southern crowd attacked the 6th Massachusetts Regiment as it marched toward Washington, prompted President Lincoln to take drastic measures. He suspended habeas corpus in several parts of the state, deployed troops in Baltimore and elsewhere, and arrested suspected Southern sympathizers, including 19 members of the legislature. Many viewed his actions as alarming examples of Federal infringements on a state's internal affairs. After the arrest of John Merryman, a suspected Confederate spy, Chief Justice Roger B. Taney held in a ruling from the Federal circuit court in Baltimore that the President could not suspend habeas corpus. Lincoln continued his policy and disregarded Taney. Meanwhile, the state legislature had voted against secession. Maryland stayed in the Union despite its divided allegiances, which persisted throughout the war.

Marylanders fought in large numbers on both sides. Out of an 1860 population numbering 515,918 whites and 171,131 blacks (83,942 of whom were free), the state provided 33,995 white soldiers, 8,718 black soldiers, and

3,925 sailors and marines to the Union cause. Approximately 20,000 white Marylanders fought for the Confederacy. The Maryland death toll in Union units totaled slightly less than 3,000, and Confederate casualties are unknown. Twelve natives of the state became Union generals and eleven attained that rank in the Confederacy. The North built its largest prison camp at Point Lookout, a grim installation with no barracks and insufficient water, on a sliver of land where the Potomac River flows into Chesapeake Bay.

More than 200 military actions took place in Maryland. Many grew out of the guerrilla skirmishes and cavalry raids that sporadically

New York State Memorial, Antietam

plagued the state. By far the most important military event was Gen. Robert E. Lee's 1862 Maryland Campaign, which led to the Battle of Antietam on September 17. A strategic disaster, the campaign battered Lee's army, frustrated Southern hopes for European recognition, cleared the way for Lincoln's preliminary proclamation of emancipation, and demonstrated that western Marylanders cared little about the Confederacy. A smaller Confederate army under Lt. Gen. Jubal A. Early entered the state in July 1864. On July 9 Early's troops defeated a motley Union force commanded by Maj. Gen. Lew Wallace at the Battle of Monocacy near Frederick.

Pressing on to Washington, Early's soldiers fired upon Fort Stevens, where President Lincoln stood viewing the action, before retiring to Virginia in mid-July.

Despite Maryland's strong pro-Confederate faction, its political leaders addressed the issue of emancipation before the war's end. In 1864 a coalition of Unionists drafted a constitutional amendment that abolished slavery. A majority of Marylanders probably opposed the amendment, but the disfranchisement of citizens who supported the Confederacy and a heavy positive vote among the state's soldiers carried the day.

ANTIETAM

The epic battle fought near the banks of Antietam Creek at Sharpsburg, Maryland, on September 17, 1862, marked the culmination of a remarkable Confederate offensive. In a little more than three months Gen. Robert E. Lee shifted the battle lines from the outskirts of Richmond to north of the Potomac River, winning two major battles in the process. His tactical defeat at Antietam, however, had profound consequences that would alter the nature and objectives of the Civil War.

Lee launched the Maryland campaign hoping to win a decisive victory against a weakened enemy. He also hoped that sympathetic Marylanders would join his depleted ranks. Moreover, a campaign on Union soil might persuade Great Britain and France to recognize the Confederacy and push for Southern independence through international diplomacy. At the very least, taking the war out of Virginia would allow the Old Dominion's farmers to harvest the crops needed to sustain the Southern army in the coming winter.

The Confederates began crossing the Potomac on September 4, but many soldiers stayed behind. Some were exhausted by months of hard campaigning; others balked at invading someone else's country. As for new recruits, wary locals in this part of Maryland favored the Union, and practically no one came forward to aid the Rebel cause. Lee's bold strike into hostile territory would be carried out with only 40,000 men or fewer.

To complicate matters, a strong Federal garrison at Harpers Ferry

◢ *132nd Pennsylvania Monument, Bloody Lane, Antietam*

BATTLE FACTS

Battle date	September 17, 1862
Combat strength	U.S. 75,000; C.S. 38,000
Casualties	U.S. 12,400; C.S. 10,300
Commanders	U.S. Maj. Gen. George B. McClellan
	C.S. Gen. Robert E. Lee

threatened Lee's supply line through the Shenandoah Valley. Abandoning his notion of a popular uprising, Lee decided to divide his modest army into four widely separated parts and encircle Harpers Ferry. Special Orders 191, which detailed his plans, went out from headquarters on September 9.

Lee adopted this risky maneuver because he knew the character of his opponent. Maj. Gen. George B. McClellan was a brilliant administrator and a profoundly cautious strategist. That month in the Army of the Potomac, he could muster some 87,000 men. But he firmly believed the Confederates

outnumbered him—just as he thought they had in the spring. Lee reasoned that he could reduce Harpers Ferry and reunite his forces before Little Mac dared move within striking range.

Then, on September 13, two Indiana soldiers lolling in a meadow discovered a copy of Special Orders 191 wrapped around three cigars. The document soon reached General McClellan, who exulted to President Lincoln, "I have the plans of the rebels, and will catch them in their own trap. Will send you trophies."

McClellan had indeed caught

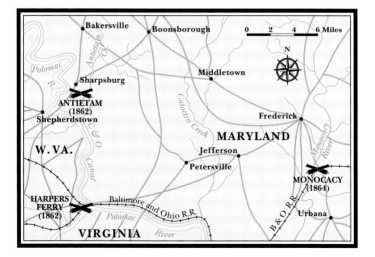

Lee in a vulnerable position, but he squandered his advantage. The Federals moved deliberately on September 14 toward the lightly defended gaps in South Mountain. In battles in three separate places, they cleared the road to Harpers Ferry and Lee's divided army.

But on September 15 the Union garrison at Harpers Ferry capitu-lated. Lee began to reunite his forces near Sharpsburg, positioning them between the village and Antietam Creek.

Now, with a major battle loom-ing, both commanders erred. Lee had nothing to gain by staying in Maryland and gambled with his army by placing it with its back to the Potomac River. Hoping Lee

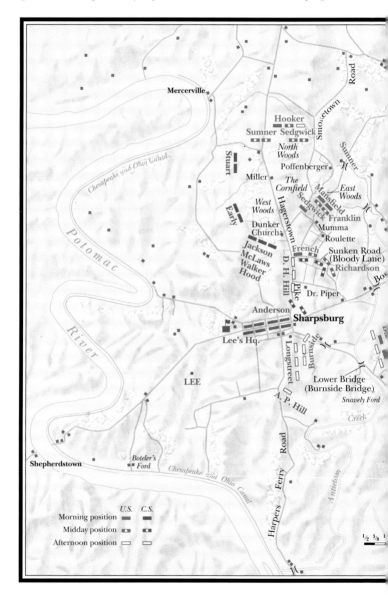

	U.S.	C.S.
Morning position		
Midday position		
Afternoon position		

would retreat to Virginia without fighting, McClellan idled away two days as the Confederate leader assembled most of his divided army. At last McClellan realized that the Rebels were not withdrawing, and he prepared to attack.

The battle General Lee had sought began about dawn on September 17. It would be the bloodiest day in American history. McClellan ordered the offensive to begin at the north end of his line, where Maj. Gen. Joseph Hooker faced one of Lee's finest officers, Maj. Gen. Thomas J. "Stonewall" Jackson. Hooker's men moved across the Miller Cornfield toward the tiny whitewashed church of a pacifist sect known as the Dunkers. The Cornfield changed hands repeatedly as soldiers in blue and gray surged back and forth through the furrows. "In the time I am writing," recalled a Union general, "every stalk of corn in the northern...part of the field was cut as closely as could have been done with a knife, and the slain lay in rows precisely as they had stood in their ranks a few moments before." When a fresh Northern division rushed recklessly toward a patch of trees known as the West Woods, unseen Confederates inflicted 2,300 casualties in 20 minutes. The Union assault ended late in the morning; Jackson's forces had held the flank—but only by the slimmest of margins.

In the center of the battlefield, the thin Confederate line occupied a sunken farm road. By day's end, the place would earn the sobriquet Bloody Lane, as wave after wave of Union attackers approached, only to be slaughtered by concealed Confederate riflemen. "My rifles flamed and roared in the Federals' faces like a blinding blaze of lightning accompanied by the quick and deadly thunderbolt," wrote a Confederate colonel. "The effect was appalling. The entire front line, with few exceptions, went down in the consuming blast."

After four Union brigades disintegrated before the Confederate

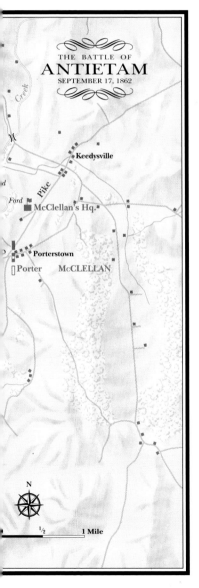

THE BATTLE OF
ANTIETAM
SEPTEMBER 17, 1862

Creek

Keedysville

Pike

Ford

McClellan's Hq.

Porterstown

Porter   McCLELLAN

N

½   1 Mile

▲ *Cornfield from North Woods, Antietam*

rifles, the Southern line began to weaken. When an Alabama officer misunderstood an order and directed his troops to withdraw from the road, Union reinforcements exploited the error. The bluecoats rushed into the lane and toward the defenseless Confederate center. But McClellan, fearing a phantom counterattack, called a halt to the pursuit. Once again, Lee's army narrowly escaped disaster.

On the south end of the field, Union troops under Maj. Gen. Ambrose E. Burnside encountered 500 Georgia riflemen defending a steep slope beyond Antietam Creek. Burnside intended to outflank the Georgians by using a downstream ford, but that effort was delayed. Insistent orders from McClellan to cross the creek left Burnside no choice but to capture the bridge immediately below the Confederate strongpoint. The Federals made three unsuccessful attempts before they could dis-

lodge their stubborn opponents and advance on Sharpsburg. The three-arched stone span won by the Union attackers is still known as Burnside's Bridge.

By midafternoon Union regiments had reached the outskirts of the village and were driving the last of Lt. Gen. James Longstreet's regiments before them. Ahead lay the Potomac River and a chance for the Federals to block the only ford by which the Army of Northern Virginia might escape annihilation. General Lee, anxiously watching the situation from a knoll near his command post, noticed new columns approaching from the south. "What troops are those?" Lee asked an officer with a telescope. "They are flying the Virginia and Confederate flags," came the welcome response. Maj. Gen. Ambrose P. Hill's division had arrived from Harpers Ferry. Hill savagely assailed Burnside's unsuspecting units and shoved the Federals back toward Antietam Creek. In so doing, he rescued the Army of Northern

Virginia from certain defeat.

When the sun set shortly after A. P. Hill's assault, nearly 23,000 American soldiers lay dead, wounded, or captured after 12 hours of combat. The Confederates remained on the field another 24 hours as Lee boldly but foolishly dared McClellan to renew the battle. Little Mac received substantial reinforcements on the morning of the 18th but declined Lee's challenge. Finally, on the night of September 18–19, the battered Rebels retreated across the Potomac. McClellan made little effort to prevent the Confederates' escape. The Battle of Antietam (known as Sharpsburg in

the South) and Lee's first Northern campaign had ended.

Many historians consider Antietam to be the true high-water mark of the Confederacy, the moment when Southern military potential peaked. As Lee marched into Maryland, Gen. Braxton Bragg commanded an imposing Rebel force in Kentucky, striving to secure that border state. After both efforts failed, Confederate strategists were increasingly confined to the defensive.

The Union, on the other hand, lost a priceless opportunity at Antietam. Never again would Lee offer his enemies such a tempting chance to destroy the Army of Northern Virginia. Almost any Union general but

▼ *Maryland State Memorial, Antietam*

McClellan would have tested Lee more rigorously, and the outcome might have shortened the Civil War.

Nevertheless, when the Confederate regiments withdrew into Virginia, prospects for British or French intervention receded as well. President Lincoln considered Antietam enough of a victory to issue a preliminary proclamation freeing Rebel-owned slaves. The proclamation redefined the war: Now the United States would wage war not only to restore the Union but to end slavery. In effect, the president had guaranteed that the nation that emerged from war would be different from the one Lincoln had inherited.

PARK INFORMATION

HEADQUARTERS: Antietam National Battlefield and Cemetery, P. O. Box 158, Sharpsburg, MD 21782. Telephone: (301) 432-5124.

DIRECTIONS: North and east of Sharpsburg, Maryland. Accessible from Md. 34 and Md. 65. Both routes intersect US 40 or 40A and I-70. Visitor Center 1 mile north of Sharpsburg or 10 miles south of Hagerstown on Md. 65.

SCHEDULE: Open daily from 8 a.m. to 6 p.m. June through August and 8:30 a.m. to 5 p.m. September through May. Closed Thanksgiving, Christmas, and New Year's Day.

ENTRANCE FEE: Ages 17–61, $1.00. Educational groups admitted free. Reservations requested.

TOURS: Self-guided tour by car, bike, or on foot follows an 8.5-mile route through battlefield past 11 tour stops. Bookstore rents or sells audiotape to accompany tour.

POINTS OF INTEREST:
■ **Antietam Visitor Center** Features museum, bookstore, research library, and 26-minute film. ■ **Antietam National Cemetery** Commemorates approximately 5,000 Union soldiers who fell on Maryland battlefields. Marker 11.

NEARBY HISTORIC INNS: Amanda's Regional Reservation Service for Bed and Breakfast, 1428 Park Ave., Baltimore, MD 21217; (410) 225-0001. Statewide reservation service for historic inns. Gettysburg, Harpers Ferry, Antietam, and Monocacy battlefields are close to each other. Inns listed for one battlefield may be convenient to others.

MONOCACY

The only Confederate general to win a major battle north of the Potomac was Lt. Gen. Jubal A. Early, and he did so in the war's last full year, when Grant had Lee pinned near Richmond and Sherman was pressing Johnston toward Atlanta. Early gained his victory on the Monocacy River near Frederick, Maryland, on July 9, 1864, during a lightning campaign in Union territory which brought him briefly to the outskirts of Washington.

Early's campaign was not in-tended to force a decisive battle, but to drive Union troops from the Shenandoah Valley and draw some of Grant's forces away from the stalemate near Richmond. Virginia's Shenandoah Valley possessed enormous significance during the Civil War. Not only was it a Confederate breadbasket, but its southwest-to-northeast configu-ration provided Southern strate-gists with a ready-made invasion corridor aimed at Washington and Baltimore. Control of the Valley always figured in the military plan-

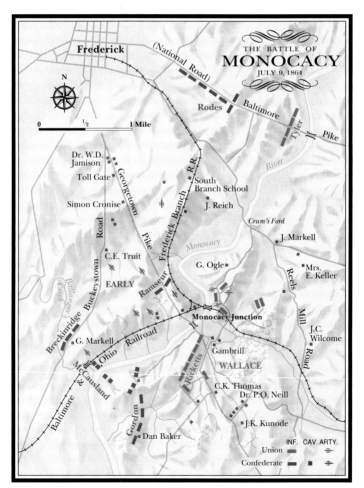

THE BATTLE OF
MONOCACY
JULY 9, 1864

Frederick

(National Road)

Rodes

Baltimore

Tyler Pike

N

0   ½   1 Mile

Dr. W.D. Jamison

Toll Gate

Georgetown Pike

R.R.

Frederick Branch

River

South Branch School

J. Reich

Crum's Ford

J. Markell

Simon Cronise

Monocacy

Mrs. E. Keller

C.E. Truit

G. Ogle

Reels

EARLY

Ramseur

Road

Buckeystown

Ball...

Creek

Breckinridge

Monocacy Junction

Mill Road

J.C. Wilcome

G. Markell

Railroad

Ohio

McCausland

Gambrill

Ricketts

WALLACE

C.K. Thomas

Dr. P.O. Neill

Baltimore

&

Gordon

Dan Baker

J.K. Kunode

INF. CAV. ARTY.

Union

Confederate

Battle date	July 9, 1864
Combat strength	U.S. 5,800; C.S. 17,000
Casualties	U.S. 1,300; C.S. 700–900
Commanders	U.S. Maj. Gen. Lewis Wallace C.S. Lt. Gen. Jubal A. Early

ning of the Union and the Confederacy.

In the late spring of 1864, Union forces under Maj. Gen. David Hunter seized control of the Valley. Then Hunter crossed the Blue Ridge Mountains, threatening to assail Richmond from the west and wreck vital Confederate rail communications. In response, General Lee detached a corps under Lt. Gen. Jubal A. Early, telling Old Jube to dispose of Hunter, then use the Valley to threaten Washington. Stonewall Jackson had done something similar in 1862 with splendid results.

Early left Cold Harbor near Richmond on June 13 with 10,000 infantry and 4,000 cavalry, promptly defeated Hunter at Lynchburg, and headed north down the Valley on June 28. The Union army in the lower Valley took refuge on Maryland Heights near Harpers Ferry, so Early simply bypassed them and crossed the Potomac on July 5 near the old Antietam battlefield. Ranging through western Maryland, his little army levied $220,000 in ransom from the region's two largest cities.

Lee's plan to make Grant weaken his stranglehold on Richmond and Petersburg worked. As Early's "invasion" progressed, Grant was compelled to send troops northward. Eight thousand men left for Baltimore and Washington on July 6, including Brig. Gen. James B. Ricketts's crack division of the Sixth Corps. Until they arrived, the Federals would have to rely on a small body of home guards and militia commanded by Maj. Gen. Lew Wallace, a 37-year-old lawyer whose reputation had never recovered from his poor showing at the Battle of Shiloh in April 1862. (Wallace is best remembered today as the author of *Ben Hur*.)

Wallace led his modest force to Monocacy Junction, east of Frederick, where roads led to both Washington and Baltimore. The Monocacy River blocked Early's path to either city. On July 8 Ricketts's division began to arrive, boosting the Federals' strength to about 6,000 men.

The following day Early approached the Monocacy and discovered the Union presence. He cautiously probed the Federal defenses at three bridges across the river. Near noon Confederate cavalry forded the river below the bridges and gained a position beyond the Union left flank.

Wallace spotted the Confederate

▲ *Thomas House, "Araby," Monocacy*

threat and sent word to Ricketts to meet the inevitable charge. When the Southerners advanced, Ricketts's veterans repulsed them twice.

Early now ordered Maj. Gen. John B. Gordon's division to follow the cavalry and turn the Union left. Gordon's seasoned soldiers went in with the Rebel yell, first striking Ricketts's left, then following with a blow to his right. The Union troops gave way. "As one of the rebels fell, it seems as if ten rose up," remembered a New Yorker. "They were within ten rods of us, firing like a sheet of flame."

While Gordon's men rolled up the south end of Wallace's line, other Confederate divisions pushed across the bridges farther north. Wallace authorized a withdrawal, and his men hurried away on the road to Baltimore. The Federals lost nearly 1,300 men during the battle, almost twice Early's casualties. The Confederates chose not to pursue their vanquished opponents because the hour was late and Early didn't want to be encumbered with prisoners. Moreover, Wallace was retreating toward Baltimore, while the Confederate general had his eyes on the Union capital.

Early arrived at the outskirts of Washington on July 11. By then more troops from Grant's army were en route to the city's fortifications. On that day President Lincoln journeyed out from the White House to observe the action. He happened to be standing on the

PARK INFORMATION

HEADQUARTERS: Monocacy National Battlefield, 4801 Urbana Pike, Frederick, MD 21701-7307. Telephone: (301) 662-3515.

DIRECTIONS: Best overall view of battlefield is from rest area south of Frederick, Maryland, off I-270 north from Washington, D.C. To reach Visitor Center continue north on 270 to I-70 and from there take Md. 355 south for 0.1 mile.

SCHEDULE: Visitor Center open daily from 8 a.m. to 4:30 p.m. Closed Thanksgiving, Christmas, and New Year's Day.

ENTRANCE FEE: None

TOURS: Currently no trails or tour roads through battlefield because much of it is still privately owned. National Park Service is acquiring land within legislative boundaries of battlefield. Araby Church Road opposite Visitor Center on Md. 355 is roughly Union forces' retreat route.

POINT OF INTEREST: **Monocacy Visitor Center** Lower level of Gambrill Mill displays Civil War artifacts.

NEARBY HISTORIC INNS: Amanda's Regional Reservation Service for Bed and Breakfast, 1428 Park Ave., Baltimore, MD 21217; (410) 225-0001. Statewide reservation service for historic inns. Gettysburg, Harpers Ferry, Antietam, and Monocacy battlefields are close to each other. Inns listed for one battlefield may be convenient to others.

parapet of Fort Stevens when Rebel bullets flew past, making him the only President in U.S. history to be fired upon in combat while in office. The reinforcements from Grant led the Confederates to cancel their attack plans that day. On July 14 Early and his men were back in Virginia.

The Battle of Monocacy is known as the engagement that saved Washington. Wallace's heroic stand delayed the Confederates by a day—time that allowed experienced Union soldiers to man the capital's defenses. Despite his failure to capture the capital, a feat which was probably beyond his powers, Early did achieve most of what Lee expected. It would take three months and 40,000 Union troops to regain permanent control of the Shenandoah Valley.

MISSISSIPPI

Mississippi fervently embraced disunion. The election of secessionist John Jones Pettus as governor in 1859 foreshadowed an early break with the North following Lincoln's election. Only South Carolina had seceded when a state convention voted 85–15 on January 9, 1861, to withdraw from the United States. Jefferson Davis, who had recently resigned as a senator from Mississippi, became president of the provisional government of the Confederacy on February 9, and Mississippi officially joined the new republic on March 29, 1861. The tide of pro-secessionist sentiment swept aside a minority of Mississippians who supported neither the Confederacy nor President Davis.

The onset of war triggered a mobilization of Mississippi's resources. From an 1860 population of 353,899 whites and 437,406 blacks (775 of whom were free), at least 75,000 whites took up arms for the Confederacy. Another 545 whites and 17,869 blacks fought for the Union. The best estimates place Confederate dead at roughly 25,000. Among leading Confederate officers born in Mississippi were Earl Van Dorn and William H. C. Whiting, who would both attain the rank of major general. Wartime manufacturing grew until the midpoint of the conflict but declined rapidly thereafter. Mississippi's industries included a large government arsenal at Columbus as well as textile mills that in late 1862 consumed 2,000 pounds of wool and 20 bales of cotton a day.

The importance of the Mississippi River in Union strategy placed Mississippi at the center of military activity during the war's first half. Before the end of hostilities more than 770 actions took place in the state. Early Union successes in Tennessee enabled an army under Maj. Gen. Henry W. Halleck to menace Corinth, a hub for transportation that endured a brief siege during May 1862 before Confederate forces under Gen. P. G. T. Beauregard evacuated the city on the 30th. Four months later, on October 3–4, costly assaults by Confederates under Maj. Gen. Earl Van Dorn failed to recapture Corinth. Confederate cavalryman Nathan Bedford Forrest operated across the state throughout the war, fighting major engagements at Brices Cross Roads on June 10,

▶ *Ruins of "Windsor," near Port Gibson*

1864, and at Tupelo on July 14–15 of that year.

The campaign for Vicksburg dwarfed all other military operations in the state. Beginning in October 1862 Maj. Gen. Ulysses S. Grant sought to capture the formidable Southern stronghold, which blocked Union control of the Mississippi River. The struggle for Vicksburg built to a climax from May to July 1863. Grant's dramatic victory at Champion Hill on May 16 served as the foundation for brilliant maneuvers that forced Confederates under Lt. Gen. John C. Pemberton into entrenchments around the city. On July 4, after a grinding six-week siege, Pemberton surrendered. Military operations in Mississippi diminished after the fall of Vicksburg, although Southern resistance continued until Lt. Gen. Richard Taylor surrendered all Confederate forces in the Department of Alabama, Mississippi, and East Louisiana on May 4, 1865, at Citronelle, Alabama.

National Historic Landmarks

CORINTH
For information, contact:
Northeast Mississippi Museum
204 4th Street East
Corinth, MS 38834
(601) 287-3120
Located 4 miles south of
Tennessee border at intersection
of US 45 and 72.

CHAMPION HILL
For information, contact:
Vicksburg Nat'l. Military Park
3201 Clay Street
Vicksburg, MS 39180
(601) 636-0583.
Located 20 miles east of
Vicksburg on I-20.

VICKSBURG

Union military strategy in the vast western theater of the Civil War hinged upon regaining control of the Mississippi River. Doing so would restore the commerce of the Ohio and northern Mississippi valleys, which depended upon the port of New Orleans. Moreover, with the Mississippi in Federal hands, Arkansas, Texas, and most of Louisiana would be isolated from the rest of the Confederacy.

In 13 months of fighting along the great river, Union forces reasserted Federal authority from the mouth of the Ohio to below Memphis, and from the Gulf of Mexico to north of Baton Rouge. By the late fall of 1862, only two strongholds remained in Southern hands: Port Hudson, Louisiana, and Vicksburg, Mississippi. President Lincoln believed that Vicksburg was "the key" and that "the war can never be brought to a close until that key is in our pocket."

Geography and transportation ensured that Vicksburg would figure largely in the struggle for the Mississippi. The prosperous town of 4,500 occupied bluffs 200 feet high, the first elevated ground along the Mississippi south of Memphis. More

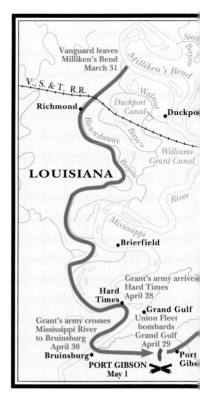

important, Vicksburg provided the only east-west rail junction with the river between Memphis and New Orleans.

Recognizing Vicksburg's significance, the Confederates turned the city into what President Jefferson Davis called the Gibraltar of

CAMPAIGN FACTS	
Campaign dates	March 29–July 4, 1863
Combat strength	U.S. 77,000; C.S. 62,000
Casualties	U.S. 10,100; C.S. 38,600 (29,500 paroled)
Commanders	U.S. Maj. Gen. Ulysses S. Grant Acting Rear Adm. David D. Porter C.S. Gen. Joseph E. Johnston Lt. Gen. John C. Pemberton

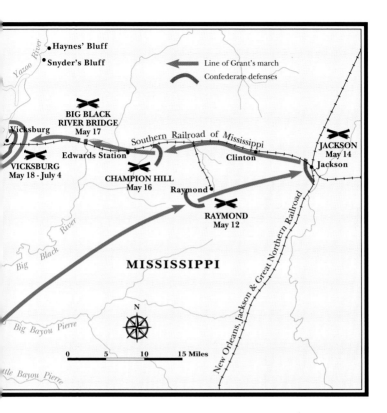

America. Engineers spent seven months perfecting an eight-mile line anchored on the river above and below the river port. Nine massive forts, some with walls 20 feet thick, covered the six wagon roads and one railroad that approached the city from the east and south. More than a hundred guns bristled from embrasures while trenches for thousands of infantry connected the forts. Swampy ground north of Vicksburg protected the defenders from those directions while powerful batteries along the river guarded the shore against Union vessels.

Lt. Gen. John C. Pemberton commanded about 50,000 Confederate troops in Mississippi. Many Southerners harbored doubts

about this native Pennsylvanian, but he enjoyed Jefferson Davis's complete confidence. Although Pemberton bore responsibility for protecting the whole state, he and Davis agreed that the defense of Vicksburg defined that task. Pemberton's immediate superior, Gen. Joseph E. Johnston, saw Confederate strategy in the West a little differently. From his headquarters in Tennessee, Johnston favored a mobile defense unfettered by concern for specific places. This difference of opinion boded ill for Confederate fortunes.

The Union commander charged with clearing the Mississippi River of Confederate resistance was Maj. Gen. Ulysses S. Grant. Grant considered the capture of

Vicksburg "a matter of first importance...equal to the amputation of a limb in its weakening effects upon the enemy." He began the campaign in west Tennessee with about 75,000 men at his disposal.

Grant's first attempt to capture Vicksburg failed in December 1862. Moving due south through Mississippi, his force of 40,000 was forced to turn back when daring Confederate cavalry raids disrupted his supply lines. A simultaneous effort by 32,000 troops under Maj. Gen. William T. Sherman approached Vicksburg via the river. Sherman's attack against the city's northern defenses ended disastrously in the marshy bottom lands fronting Chickasaw Bayou and Walnut Hills.

Undaunted, Grant spent the winter on what he termed "experiments" to reach the dry ground east of the city. Four separate amphibious operations, two in Louisiana and two in Mississippi, achieved no tangible results. But the labor kept the troops busy

while floodwaters receded and Grant plotted his spring campaign.

Grant's plan entailed dividing his large army. Leaving Sherman north of Vicksburg, he would take two corps, commanded by Maj. Gen. James McPherson and Maj. Gen. John A. McClernand (a political appointee), and march down the west side of the river. Crossing well downstream from Vicksburg, they would move south toward another Union force under Maj. Gen. Nathaniel P. Banks. Together the two armies would reduce Port Hudson, then turn north and tackle Vicksburg. Rear Adm. David D. Porter would guide his fleet down the Mississippi past the Vicksburg batteries to provide supplies and transport across the river.

On March 31, 1863, Grant began his arduous march from Milliken's Bend north of Vicksburg, arriving at Hard Times Landing some 60 river miles south of the city on April 28. On the night of April 16 Porter ran 11 vessels past the Vicksburg defenses. In order to distract Pemberton's attention from these moves, Grant ordered Sherman to feint toward the city's northern approaches and sent Col. Benjamin Grierson to lead a flashy cavalry raid south through Mississippi. These diversions worked perfectly. Even when Porter unsuccessfully bombarded the stubborn Confederate outpost at Grand Gulf opposite Hard Times Landing, Pemberton remained unsure where the real Union threat lay.

A slave informed Grant of a road leading to an alternative

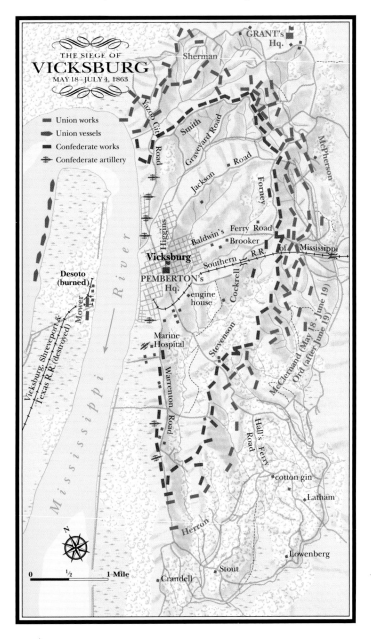

THE SIEGE OF
VICKSBURG
MAY 18 - JULY 4, 1863

- Union works
- Union vessels
- Confederate works
- Confederate artillery

crossing downstream at Bruinsburg, and on April 30–May 1 the Union army was ferried across the Mississippi unopposed. Grant wrote later that he experienced "a degree of relief scarcely ever equaled since….All the campaigns, labors, hardships, and exposures, from the month of December previous to this time…were for the accomplishment of this one object."

At this point, Grant made the key decision in the Vicksburg campaign. Banks sent word that he would be delayed in the joint movement against Port Hudson, and Grant opted to strike out on his own. Vicksburg would be his target, but first he would disperse Confederate troops near Jackson, the Mississippi capital, 45 miles to the east. By doing this, he would cut Pemberton's communications to the east and block reinforcements under Johnston from moving directly to Vicksburg's relief. But Grant's decision involved great risk; he was placing himself between two enemy armies.

As the Federals began to march inland from Bruinsburg, 8,000 Confederates under Brig. Gen. John S. Bowen advanced from Grand Gulf and Vicksburg to oppose them. On May 1 a sharp battle at Port Gibson, 30 miles south of Vicksburg, forced Bowen's outnumbered men back, and Grant gained higher ground east of the river. Waiting until Sherman's corps arrived from its successful ploy north of Vicksburg, Grant resumed his march on May 7 with an army of 45,000. Confused by the abundance of seemingly contradictory Union initiatives and wedded to the direct defense of Vicksburg, Pemberton pulled in his forces and looked for Grant to move north toward the city.

Grant's advance toward Jackson met no resistance save for a single Confederate brigade under Brig. Gen. John Gregg, part of the makeshift army forming under Johnston's direction. A portion of McPherson's corps brushed aside Gregg at Raymond, 15 miles southwest of Jackson, on May 12. The following day Johnston himself reached Jackson to discover only 6,000 troops present for duty. Recognizing that reinforcements would arrive too late to save the capital, Johnston ordered his men to fight a delaying action while supplies were removed. On May 14 McPherson and Sherman attacked and by 4 p.m. the city was in Union hands. Johnston and his troops escaped to the north.

Johnston had ordered Pemberton to move out of the Vicksburg trenches and attack Grant's rear. At the head of 22,000 troops, Pemberton slowly advanced east along the road leading to Jackson and took position on a prominent knoll called Champion Hill. On May 16 McPherson and McClernand with 29,000 men between them met Pemberton in the bloodiest battle of the Vicksburg Campaign. Neither side displayed brilliant generalship at Champion Hill although the fighting was "one of the most obstinate and murderous conflicts of the war," according to a Union officer. In the end the Federals prevailed, inflicting nearly 4,000 casualties on Pemberton, not counting a division that became separated from his army and drifted off eventually to join Johnston. The Unionists lost 2,500 men. The next day Pemberton fought a rearguard action at a bridge on the Big Black River just 12 miles east of Vicksburg. In this

▲ *National Cemetery, Vicksburg*

costly engagement, the Federals captured 1,700 Confederate soldiers and 18 guns. The rest of Pemberton's force limped west into Vicksburg.

Grant's campaign in Mississippi had thus far been a spectacular success. For 18 days his army had moved through hostile country while winning five engagements and keeping Johnston and Pemberton apart. Now all that remained was to take Vicksburg. Believing the Confederates to be demoralized by their reverses, Grant ordered a frontal assault against the trenches on May 19. The greeting he received shocked him; a thousand bluecoats fell during the attack. Pemberton's army, reinvigorated by the strength of their defenses and the esprit of two fresh divisions who had not fought at Champion Hill, repulsed Grant with ease. Grant renewed his offensive on the 22nd, only to meet the same tragic results. "It was a tornado of iron on our left, a hurricane of shot on our right,"

wrote a Federal soldier. "We passed through the mouth of hell. Every third man fell, either killed or wounded." Grant was now convinced that his offensive was stymied. "We'll have to dig our way in," he reluctantly concluded.

While Pemberton's 30,000 troops manned their parapets and consumed an ever-dwindling stockpile of food, Grant mounted more than 200 cannon with which he shelled the city and its protectors day and night. Porter's fleet added to the terror by lobbing tons of iron at Vicksburg from the water. Vicksburg's civilians huddled in their homes or sought shelter in makeshift caves.

As the siege continued, Federal soldiers relentlessly dug a series of approach trenches which gradually brought the opposing lines within a few yards of one another. On two occasions Union troops detonated mines under Confederate strongpoints, but in neither case did this dramatic tactic permanently rupture the line. Nevertheless, Grant's siege became so effective that, as one historian has written, "a cat could not have crept out of Vicksburg without being discovered." Reinforcements from Missouri, Kentucky, and Tennessee raised Grant's strength to 77,000. This allowed him to establish a new defensive line facing east, neutralizing Johnston's growing army.

On July 1 Pemberton questioned his division commanders as to their views on whether they should attempt to break the siege. Relief from Johnston could not be expected, and the garrison faced certain starvation unless they escaped from the city. But 10,000 soldiers lay sick or wounded and the rest were too weak, said three of the four Confederate generals, to sustain an offensive. This left no option but surrender.

Pemberton met Grant on July 3 to discuss the capitulation of his garrison. Grant offered no terms but unconditional surrender, a proposal Pemberton declined. The Union leader then modified his position to allow for the parole of Confederate soldiers. Pemberton agreed, and on July 4 Vicksburg raised the white flag.

The 47-day siege ended one of the most important chapters of the Civil War. Confederate general Stephen D. Lee called the capture of Vicksburg "a staggering blow from which the Confederacy never rallied." Vicksburg's demise isolated Port Hudson and rendered its continued defense meaningless. The commanders agreed upon a truce which led to a Confederate surrender on July 9. On July 16 the first vessel to travel from the north in two years docked at New Orleans. A grateful President Lincoln remarked, "The Father of Waters again goes unvexed to the sea."

PARK INFORMATION

HEADQUARTERS: Vicksburg National Military Park, 3201 Clay St., Vicksburg, MS 39180. Telephone: (601) 636-0583.

DIRECTIONS: Located in northeastern Vicksburg, park entrance and Visitor Center are on Clay Street (US 80) within 1 mile of I-20.

SCHEDULE: Grounds open daily until dark. Visitor Center and USS *Cairo* Museum open daily from 8 a.m. to 5 p.m. and 9 a.m. to 5 p.m., respectively. Closed Christmas.

ENTRANCE FEE: $3 per vehicle, $1 per bus passenger; U.S. citizens over 62 and school groups free.

TOURS: Visitors should begin 16-mile self-guided auto tour at Visitor Center where exhibits and film explain Vicksburg campaign. Fifteen wayside markers provide interpretive information.

POINTS OF INTEREST:
■ **USS *Cairo* Museum** Houses more than 1,000 maritime artifacts and offers audiovisual presentation.
■ **Vicksburg National Cemetery** Marker 8.

NEARBY HISTORIC INNS: Lincoln, Ltd., Mississippi Bed and Breakfast Reservation Service, P. O. Box 3479, Meridian, MS 39303; (601) 482-5483 or (800) 633-6477. Statewide reservation service for historic inns.

BRICES CROSS ROADS

In the late spring of 1864, Maj. Gen. William T. Sherman led three Union armies into Georgia on a campaign to capture Atlanta and destroy the Confederate forces defending the city. Sherman's offensive relied on a single-track railroad that led between Atlanta and Nashville, Tennessee. Without a secure supply line, "the Atlanta Campaign was an impossibility," said the Union commander.

Maj. Gen. Nathan Bedford Forrest, known as the Wizard of the Saddle, worried Sherman. "I expect to hear every day of Forrest breaking into Tennessee from some quarter," he wrote. "Forrest is a…dangerous man."

Sherman was right. Forrest left his base in northern Mississippi on June 1 heading for the Union rail lines in Tennessee. He had reached Russellville, Alabama, when he received word from his immediate superior, Maj. Gen. Stephen D. Lee, to return to Mississippi and meet a new Federal force moving east from Memphis.

Brig. Gen. Samuel D. Sturgis, a 41-year-old West Pointer and commander of Union cavalry in the Military District of West Tennessee, led these Northerners, a force of 8,100 men and 22 guns. The Union cavalry left Lafayette on June 2 with orders to seek out and destroy Forrest's cavalry. Delayed by heavy rains and muddy roads, they slogged south through Mississippi toward Forrest's haunts around Tupelo. By June 9 Sturgis had reached a point south of Ripley and nine miles north of an intersection called Brices Cross Roads.

Forrest returned to Tupelo on June 5 and deployed his four brigades of troopers, numbering some 3,500 men, to cover all possible Union approaches. As Sturgis pushed deeper into Mississippi, Forrest developed a plan to defeat him. The Confederates would strike at Brices Cross Roads, counting on surprise and the area's thick vegetation to compensate for their inferior numbers. Forrest uncannily predicted the actual course of combat: "Their cavalry will move out ahead of their infantry and should reach the crossroads three hours in advance. We can whip their cavalry in that time. As soon as the fight opens they will send back to have the infantry hurried in. It is going to be hot as hell, and coming on the run for five or six miles, their infantry will be so tired out that we will ride right over them."

That is almost exactly what

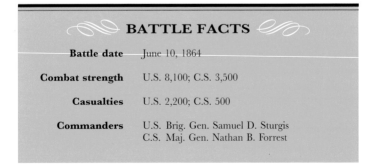

✇ BATTLE FACTS ✇

Battle date	June 10, 1864
Combat strength	U.S. 8,100; C.S. 3,500
Casualties	U.S. 2,200; C.S. 500
Commanders	U.S. Brig. Gen. Samuel D. Sturgis C.S. Maj. Gen. Nathan B. Forrest

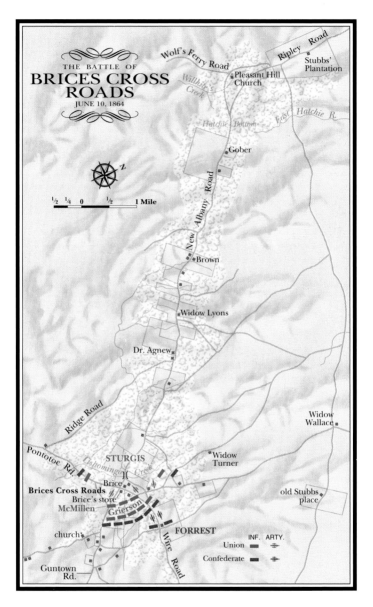

THE BATTLE OF
BRICES CROSS ROADS
JUNE 10, 1864

Wolf's Ferry Road

Ripley Road

Stubbs' Plantation

Pleasant Hill Church

Willhite Creek

East Hatchie R.

Hatchie Bottom

Gober

New Albany Road

1/2 1/4 0 1/2 1 Mile

Brown

Widow Lyons

Dr. Agnew

Ridge Road

Widow Wallace

Pontotoc Rd.

STURGIS

Tishomingo Creek

Widow Turner

Brice

old Stubbs place

Brices Cross Roads

Brice's store

McMillen

Grierson

FORREST

church

Wire Road

Guntown Rd.

INF. ARTY.
Union
Confederate

happened. On June 10 Sturgis sent his cavalry under Brig. Gen. Benjamin Grierson to seize the junction at Brices. By 9:45 a.m. the Union horsemen controlled the forks and the countryside around them. Forrest appeared somewhat later with his vanguard, launching a series of probes that pinned down Grierson. Sturgis arrived at noon and quickly ordered Col. William L. McMillen's infantry to rush to the crossroads.

By 1 p.m. most of Forrest's troopers had arrived. His attack pushed back Grierson's weary men, whose ammunition began to run out. However, two of McMillen's brigades appeared by 2 p.m. and stabilized the Union line. Now Forrest prepared for his final assault. "Every man must charge and we will give them hell," he directed. The Confederates galloped headlong into the blue lines, precipitating a fierce two-hour fight. But when Forrest turned both Union flanks, Sturgis's line collapsed.

"Order gave way to confusion and confusion to panic," lamented Sturgis. "Everywhere the army now drifted toward the rear, and was soon altogether beyond control." When a wagon overturned on a narrow bridge across Tishomingo Creek, the Union withdrawal turned into a rout. Artillery, ambulances, caissons, and demoralized troops jammed the roadway. Forrest instructed his victorious men to "keep the skeer on 'em," and the pursuit continued for three miles until darkness shielded the fleeing Federals.

The distraught Sturgis cried, "For God's sake, if Mr. Forrest will let me alone, I will let him alone," but Mr. Forrest would not be a party to such a bargain. At 1 a.m. on June 11 the Confederates renewed their pursuit, and Sturgis's column did not stop backpedaling until it reached the outskirts of Memphis nearly 90 miles northeast of Brices Cross Roads.

The Battle of Brices Cross Roads was a complete Confederate tactical victory. Sturgis suffered heavy losses: 617 killed or wounded and some 1,600 taken prisoner. Forrest, fighting twice his number, reported 492 casualties. But in a larger sense, Sturgis still accomplished Sherman's goal. Lee instructed Forrest to remain in Mississippi rather than raid the Tennessee railroads as long as the Magnolia State was threatened with invasion. This kind of strategic thinking often obscured the military priorities of the Confederacy. Sherman's capture of Atlanta less than three months later proved to be a devastating blow to Southern independence.

PARK INFORMATION

HEADQUARTERS: National Park Service, Natchez Trace Parkway, R. R. 1, NT 143, Tupelo, MS 38801. Telephone: (601) 680-4025.

DIRECTIONS: Located on Miss. 370, 6 miles west of Baldwin. No visitor center at battlefield site, but park interpreters at Natchez Trace Parkway Visitor Center at Milepost 266 on parkway can provide information about battle.

SCHEDULE: Visitor Center open daily from 8 a.m. to 5 p.m. Closed Christmas.

POINTS OF INTEREST: **Tupelo Convention & Visitors Bureau** Located in Tupelo on East Main St. adjacent to Coliseum. Brochures available on battle of Brices Cross Roads and nearby points of interest.

NEARBY HISTORIC INNS: Lincoln, Ltd., Mississippi Bed and Breakfast Reservation Service, P. O. Box 3479, Meridian, MS 39303; (601) 482-5483 or (800) 633-6477. Statewide reservation service for historic inns.

TUPELO

The Confederate victory at Brices Cross Roads did not end the contest between Nathan Bedford Forrest and Union forces charged with protecting supply lines through middle Tennessee. As Sherman moved ever closer to Atlanta, the safety of his rail communications to the north grew more critical. Sherman intended to trap "that devil Forrest" in northern Mississippi, he wrote, "if it costs 10,000 lives and breaks the Treasury. There will never be peace in Tennessee till Forrest is dead." The Union commander concluded, "If we do not punish Forrest and the people now, the whole effect of our past conquests will be lost."

He assigned this task to Maj. Gen. Andrew Jackson Smith, a Pennsylvanian and nails-tough career soldier who had led a division during the Vicksburg campaign and arrived in Mississippi from the aborted Red River Campaign in Louisiana. Smith commanded two infantry divisions, a brigade of black troops, a division of cavalry, and 28 guns. Smith's immediate superior believed that these 14,000 bluecoats could "whip anything this side of Georgia." On July 5 Smith left La Grange, Tennessee, moving south through Mississippi and heeding Sherman's wishes to visit destruction on civilian

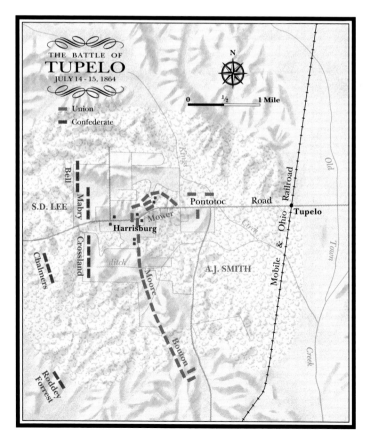

BATTLE FACTS

Battle dates	July 14–15, 1864
Combat strength	U.S. 14,000; C.S. 9,500
Casualties	U.S. 700; C.S. 1,400
Commanders	U.S. Maj. Gen. Andrew J. Smith C.S. Lt. Gen. Stephen D. Lee Maj. Gen. Nathan B. Forrest

resources. The Federals reached Pontotoc on July 11; a swath of destruction ten miles wide lay in their wake.

Forrest knew of the Union depredations but had orders from Lt. Gen. Stephen D. Lee, a native South Carolinian and former artillery commander at Vicksburg, not to risk attacking Smith's column until Lee could bring reinforcements to bear. When the Southern forces united at Okolona, they totaled nearly 9,500 men.

Fearing an ambush as Confederate resistance intensified, Smith veered sharply east on July 13, Forrest's 43rd birthday, and took a position on the Mobile & Ohio Railroad near Tupelo. Now in charge of the Confederate army, Stephen Lee pursued the Yankees, anxious to defeat them as soon as possible. He had heard reports of a Union column heading toward Mobile, Alabama, the South's most important Gulf port, and wished to detach some of his men to protect that city. But first he had to deal with Smith. On the night of July 13 the Confederates found their opponents entrenched on an open ridge two miles west of Tupelo near the village of Harrisburg. Smith's fishhook line impressed Forrest as "naturally strong [and]…almost impreg-

nable." Lee made preparations for an attack the next morning.

Lee and Forrest intended to hit the Union line in several places simultaneously, but a Kentucky brigade jumped the gun and charged alone at about 7:30 a.m. Their repulse set the tone for the rest of the morning as piecemeal attacks, described by one Confederate as "all gallantry and useless sacrifice," first assailed the Union left, then tried the right.

The battle "seemed to be a footrace to see who should reach us first," remembered Smith. "They were allowed to approach, yelling and howling like Comanches, to within canister range…. They would come forward and fall back, rally and forward again…. Their determination may be seen from the fact that their dead were found within thirty yards of our batteries." The Confederate veterans fought dismounted for two and a half hours, but the Federals would not break. "Human beings could not stand such a storm," wrote one witness, and when some of Smith's men counterattacked, the Confederates withdrew to a fortified line of their own.

The battlefield remained quiet until after dark. Then Forrest attempted to envelop the Union left flank, an initiative that flatly failed. The next morning the Confederates renewed the attack with a single brigade; Smith's Federals turned it back. "But few men were killed or wounded in this engagement," reported Forrest, "but I found the road strewn with men fainting under the oppressive heat, hard labor, and want of water." In spite of his successful defense, Smith decided to abandon the area and return to Memphis. Some of his supplies had spoiled in the merciless Mississippi sun, and his ammunition supply had dwindled dangerously. At midday the Federals pulled out, presenting the curious spectacle of a victorious and numerically superior army retreating before a beaten foe. Characteristically Forrest pursued, and paid for his aggression with a painful foot wound that knocked him out of action. The combat gradually diminished, and by July 23 Smith was back in Memphis.

The fighting at Tupelo produced mixed results. Tactically, the Union army "defeated Forrest as he had never been defeated before," wrote W. S. Burns, a captain in the 4th Missouri Cavalry. The Confederates suffered 1,373 casualties in the campaign, nearly twice the Union total. Smith's soldiers performed well, including the black brigade, which "fought excellently…and showed the effect of discipline and drill." Smith went on to admit that "their action has removed from my mind a prejudice of twenty years' standing."

On the other hand, Smith's retreat tarnished his triumph and his failure to destroy Forrest displeased Sherman. The sideshow in Mississippi would continue as long as Sherman required a secure railroad behind him. Forrest confessed that driving the Federals away from Tupelo "cost the best blood of the South" and delayed his interdiction of the Union supply line until Atlanta had fallen. He would, however, continue to vex Sherman for the rest of the year, until the main Confederate army in the west bled itself dry at Franklin and Nashville, Tennessee.

PARK INFORMATION

HEADQUARTERS: National Park Service, Natchez Trace Parkway, R. R. 1, NT 143, Tupelo, MS 38801. Telephone: (601) 680-4025.

DIRECTIONS: Located within city limits of Tupelo on Miss. 6, about 1 mile west of US 45 (business). East of Natchez Trace Parkway by 1.2 miles. Site is near where Confederate line formed to attack Union position. No visitor center at battlefield site, but park interpreters at Natchez Trace Parkway Visitor Center at Milepost 266 on parkway can provide information about battle.

SCHEDULE: Visitor Center open daily from 8 a.m. to 5 p.m. Closed Christmas.

POINT OF INTEREST: **Tupelo Convention & Visitors Bureau** Located in Tupelo on East Main St. adjacent to Coliseum. Brochures available on battle of Tupelo and nearby points of interest.

NEARBY HISTORIC INNS: Lincoln, Ltd., Mississippi Bed and Breakfast Reservation Service, P. O. Box 3479, Meridian, MS 39303; (601) 482-5483 or (800) 633-6477. Statewide reservation service for historic inns.

MISSOURI

issouri suffered enormous internal strife during the Civil War. Influenced by years of sectional violence in neighboring Kansas, Missourians confronted the crisis of 1860 with deeply divided loyalties. The state supported moderates John Bell and Stephen A. Douglas in that year's presidential election, yet chose secessionist Claiborne F. Jackson as governor. Although a majority of whites approved of slavery (slaves made up slightly more than 10 percent of the population), growing industrial and commercial ties bound Missouri to the North. Political strife during 1861 pitted Unionists centered in St. Louis against Jackson and his supporters. A state convention voted against secession in March, after which Jackson, who continued his secessionist crusade, was removed from office. A rump government headed by Jackson gained admission to the Confederacy in November 1861. Although a star was added to the Confederate flag to mark this event, the state remained in the Union throughout the war.

Enlistments from Missouri underscored internal dissension. Home to 1,062,555 whites, 114,931 slaves, and 3,572 free blacks, the state contributed 100,616 white and 8,344 black soldiers to the Union and at least 30,000 whites to the Confederacy. An additional 3,000 Missourians became Confederate guerrillas. Deaths totaled 13,885 among Union troops and probably approached 7,500 among Confeder-

ates. Missourians who played prominent roles in the war included Confederate Maj. Gen. Sterling Price, Union Maj. Gen. Francis Preston Blair, Jr., and Montgomery Blair and Edward Bates, both of whom served in Lincoln's cabinet.

More than 1,150 military events took place in Missouri. The first notable encounter came on May 10, 1861, when Federal units commanded by Capt. Nathaniel Lyon seized pro-Confederate militiamen at Camp Jackson near St. Louis, thereby frustrating efforts to reach a peaceful accommodation in the state. A Southern army under Brig. Gen. Ben McCulloch

David Muench

▶ *Wilson's Creek*

defeated Federals under Lyon at Wilson's Creek on August 10, 1861. Chances for significant Confederate military success in Missouri were extinguished, however, by the Union victory at Pea Ridge, Arkansas, on March 7–8, 1862. Price mounted a last attempt to impose Confederate control on the state in the fall of 1864, sustaining a decisive defeat at Westport, near Kansas City, on October 23.

Guerrilla warfare cursed Missouri from the opening of hostilities and escalated to a level unknown in any other state. In many ways these raids and skirmishes were an extension of prewar strife between free-soil and pro-slavery elements in Kansas. Guerrilla operations in Missouri provided an arena for such notorious characters as Confederates William C. Quantrill and "Bloody Bill" Anderson, not to mention Col. Charles R. Jennison, a Union colonel whose Jayhawkers were described by a friendly witness as "*a band of destroying angels….* [who] take no prisoners and are not troubled with red tape sentimentalism in any form." This aspect of the war in Missouri displaced thousands of civilians, disrupted the agricultural and industrial development of much of the state, and contributed to continuing bloodshed during the postwar years.

WILSON'S CREEK

Following the surrender of Fort Sumter and President Abraham Lincoln's subsequent call for volunteers to suppress the rebellion, four states from the upper South joined their seven Dixie neighbors in secession from the Union. This left the remaining slave states, Delaware, Maryland, Kentucky, and Missouri, to contemplate the Confederacy's invitation to cast their fates with their Southern friends. Of the four, Missouri possessed the most importance.

Missouri's strategic location on two major waterways, the Missouri and Mississippi Rivers, and its abundant manpower and natural resources, made it a coveted military prize for both sides. To a large degree Missouri's course would determine Kentucky's decision. Their borders met along the Mississippi, and secessionists and Unionists populated both states in near-equal proportions.

Missouri's governor, Claiborne F. Jackson, sided with the Confederacy and responded in no uncertain terms to Lincoln's call for four regiments to fight the rebels: "Your requisition is illegal, unconstitutional, revolutionary…inhuman, diabolical, and cannot be complied with." Jackson gathered the secession-minded Missouri State Militia outside St. Louis, where he hoped to seize a rich cache of arms and ammunition from the Federal arsenal.

The arsenal's commander, a 42-year-old Regular Army captain named Nathaniel Lyon, despised secessionists with "an anger that was almost insane." With the help of Missouri congressman Frank Blair, Lyon organized 3,000 Home Guards loyal to the Union and surrounded the governor's outnumbered force. He thus erased the immediate threat to St. Louis, but his gloves-off action ended Missouri's slim hope of settling its destiny peacefully.

Lyon, now a brigadier general, then embarked on a military campaign to secure Missouri for the Union, and his course took him into the southwestern part of the state, where Maj. Gen. Sterling Price was mustering pro-Confederate Missourians into an army. Price had served as governor and congressman and had fought in the Mexican War. At his camp 75 miles southwest of Springfield, he assembled some 7,000 recruits, many of whom had neither uniforms nor firearms.

By July 13 Lyon had reached

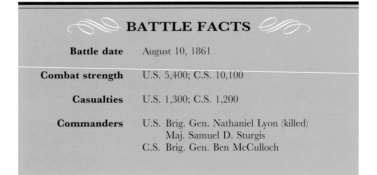

BATTLE FACTS

Battle date	August 10, 1861
Combat strength	U.S. 5,400; C.S. 10,100
Casualties	U.S. 1,300; C.S. 1,200
Commanders	U.S. Brig. Gen. Nathaniel Lyon (killed) Maj. Samuel D. Sturgis C.S. Brig. Gen. Ben McCulloch

Springfield with about 6,000 troops from Missouri, Kansas, Iowa, and the Regular Army. Here he drilled his men who, for the most part, were better armed but no more experienced than Price's soldiers. Lyon left Springfield at the end of the month, marching south to destroy Price. On the way he met the Confederate vanguard moving toward him and discovered that Brig. Gen. Benjamin McCulloch, a former Texas Ranger commanding 5,000 Confederate troops from Arkansas, Louisiana, and Texas, had joined forces with Price. After a few skirmishes with the Rebels, who vastly outnumbered his command, Lyon withdrew to Springfield. The Confederates pursued and on August 6 went into camp along Wilson's Creek ten miles to the southwest.

The Federal commander now confronted a dilemma. Springfield offered no particular defensive advantages, and Lyon's supply line stretched 120 miles northeast to the railhead at Rolla. To remain would court disaster, but to retreat without adequate cavalry protection promised no better results. In consultation with Col. Franz Sigel, Lyon decided to launch a daring attack. Sigel would lead 1,200 men on a wide sweep to the south and surprise the Confederate rear while Lyon marched the main body of his army, 4,200 troops, against the enemy front. A rearguard of 1,000 Unionists would remain in Springfield. Lyon set the attack for August 10, using a night march to sneak into position. Before his eager men moved out, Lyon told them they were in for a battle: "Fire low—don't aim higher than their knees; wait until they get

close; don't get scared; it's no part of a soldier's duty to get scared."

Price and McCulloch had also planned an offensive for August 10, but rain on the night of the ninth prompted them to cancel their plans. No one remembered to post new pickets around the perimeters of the Confederate camp, so Lyon crept close to the slumbering enemy without being seen. The battle opened about 5 a.m., when Lyon's troops swept down on the Confederates west of Wilson's Creek and pushed forward to a 150-foot-high spur called Oak Hill. Price stabilized his line on the south slope of this ridge and both sides brought up artillery.

Lyon sent Capt. Joseph B. Plummer with a battalion of Home Guards and 300 Regulars to the east side of the creek to secure the flank. Plummer soon found a Confederate battery with infantry support firing on Lyon's troops. Plummer attacked, but a bitter hour-long fight failed to clear the east side of the creek of Confederate resistance.

Meanwhile, Sigel's flanking column had gone into position farther south before dawn, placing a battery on high ground east of the creek. When he heard Lyon's guns, Sigel also opened fire. The unexpected bombardment scattered the drowsy Confederate cavalry and Sigel crossed the creek in pursuit. Rallying his troops in this sector, McCulloch sent them raging back at Sigel. "Captain, take your company up and give them hell," McCulloch ordered a Louisiana officer. At this early stage of the war, units wore all manner of uniforms. Sigel mistook a gray-clad Louisiana regiment for an Iowa outfit that also wore gray and ordered his men not to fire at the approaching figures. This error allowed the Confederates a free volley. Sigel's stunned men broke and ran, abandoning five cannon to the Confederates.

With Sigel out of the fight, the battle focused on Lyon's position, soon to be known as Bloody Hill.

Maj. John M. Schofield, Lyon's chief of staff, said that when the entire Confederate army turned on Lyon, "the engagement at once became general and almost inconceivably fierce along the entire line." Trying to drive Lyon from the high ground, Price orchestrated no fewer than three distinct charges. "You will soon be in a

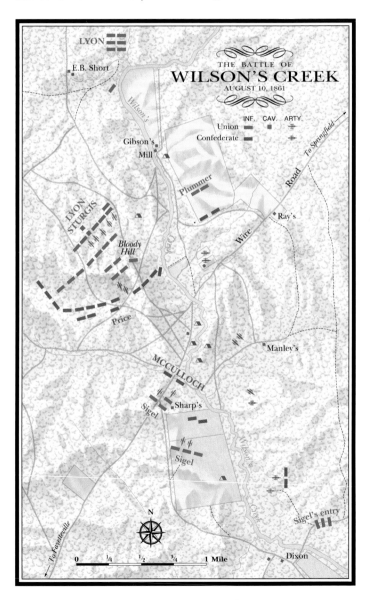

THE BATTLE OF
WILSON'S CREEK
AUGUST 10, 1861

pretty hot place," Price counseled his lead units. "Keep cool as the inside of a cucumber and give them thunder." Col. Thomas L. Snead, a staff officer serving with Price, remembered that "the lines would approach again and again within less than 50 yards of each other and then, after delivering a deadly fire, each would fall back a few paces to reform and reload, only to advance again, and again renew this strange battle in the woods."

Despite suffering wounds to the head and leg, Lyon continued to direct the battle with inspiration, waving his sword and cheering on his men who held their positions through sheer determination and efficiency of the Union artillery. The Union commander was in the act of leading a counterattack when a bullet slammed into his chest and killed him almost instantly. Maj. Samuel D. Sturgis succeeded Lyon, repulsing yet another Confederate assault late in the morning. But Sturgis worried that his exhausted men could not fight much longer. With Sigel defeated, he knew that the odds had turned against him. Sturgis ordered a retreat and the tired Confederates, disorganized and low on ammunition, allowed him to escape unmolested.

Although the 1,300 and 1,200 losses on each side seem small by late-war standards, the Battle of Wilson's Creek (known as Oak Hills in the South) proved to be one of the most vicious engagements of the Civil War. Fifteen percent of all troops engaged became casualties. Wilson's Creek also served as a proving ground for leadership. No fewer than 30 future Union major or brigadier generals participated in the battle.

The Federals lost the battle but crippled the Confederate army sufficiently to prevent it from mounting a serious effort to control the state. With every passing month, Missouri settled more firmly within the Union sphere, a process that would be concluded the following March at the Battle of Pea Ridge.

PARK INFORMATION

HEADQUARTERS: Wilson's Creek National Battlefield, Route 2, Box 75, Republic, MO 65738. Telephone: (417) 732-2662.

DIRECTIONS: Located 3 miles east of Republic and 10 miles southwest of Springfield. From I-44, take Mo. MM south for 6 miles. Turn right onto Mo. ZZ, and proceed 2 miles to park entrance.

SCHEDULE: Open daily from 8 a.m. to 5 p.m. in winter; from 8 a.m. to 7 p.m. in spring and fall; and from 8 a.m. to 9 p.m. in summer. Closed Christmas and New Year's Day.

ENTRANCE FEE: Ages 17 to 61, $1.00.

TOURS: Self-guided tour follows 4.9-mile route past wayside exhibits at 8 tour stops. Guided group tours must be prearranged with park.

POINT OF INTEREST: **Visitor Center** Features film, battle map, and museum.

NEARBY HISTORIC INNS: The Mansion at Elfindale (1892), Springfield; (417) 831-5400. Walnut Street Inn (1894), Springfield; (417) 864-6346.

NEW MEXICO

T he sprawling New Mexico Territory drew the attention of Confederates who considered it a gateway to commercial growth. "The Federals have us surrounded and utterly shut [off]…from commerce with the Pacific as well as with Northern Mexico," observed one Southern newspaper: "We must have and keep…[New Mexico] at all hazards." The territory comprised present-day New Mexico and Arizona, together with Nevada's southern tip. The 1860 census, which did not include Native Americans, recorded a population of 93,516. Most were of Mexican descent. A majority of the inhabitants were clustered along the Rio Grande River, and Santa Fe, a town of nearly 5,000, served as capital of the territory and southwestern terminus for the famous trade route that bore its name.

Although only 20 or 30 slaves lived in New Mexico in 1860, the territorial legislature had passed a slave code in 1859 that showed its affinity with the slaveholding South. Most New Mexicans south of the 34th parallel, a part of the territory then known as Arizona, favored the Confederacy. Above the 34th parallel, the population depended on trade with Northern states and remained loyal to the Union.

In special elections held during the spring of 1861, residents of Tucson and of the Mesilla Valley north of El Paso voted to join the Confederacy. This gesture lacked the force of law but nonetheless sent a clear signal to Confederates in Texas. A small column of Texans under Lt. Col. John R. Baylor pushed Union soldiers out of the Mesilla Valley in July 1861, after which Baylor christened the area below the 34th parallel the Territory of Arizona and set up a provisional government with himself as military governor. On January 24, 1862, the Confederate Congress made Baylor's actions official and seated a delegate from Arizona.

A larger Confederate force commanded by Brig. Gen. Henry Hopkins Sibley penetrated far into New Mexico in early 1862, hoping

▶ *Southeast from near top of pass, Glorieta*

to conquer the entire territory and perhaps move into Colorado. On February 21 Sibley's troops took part in a sharp action at Valverde near Fort Craig on the Rio Grande; during the first week in March, they occupied Albuquerque and Santa Fe. On March 26 part of Sibley's command fought inconclusively with a force of Colorado volunteers under Maj. John M. Chivington at Apache Canyon, where the Santa Fe Trail crossed the Sangre de Cristo Mountains some 20 miles southeast of Santa Fe. Two days later Sibley's campaign reached a climax nearby in the Battle of Glorieta Pass. Despite winning a tactical victory at Glorieta, the Confederates faced supply problems that compelled their withdrawal from New Mexico.

Sibley's departure ended a brief season of Confederate control in Arizona, after which the New Mexico Territory remained a loyal Union backwater. Before the end of the conflict, 6,561 New Mexicans served in the Union army and 277 of these men died. An undetermined number fought for the Confederacy.

GLORIETA PASS

In the summer of 1861 President Jefferson Davis ordered Brig. Gen. Henry Hopkins Sibley to recruit an army of Texans for the purpose of establishing a Confederate New Mexico and opening a way to the Colorado mines, California, and the Pacific Ocean. Sibley, a hard-drinking West Pointer, gathered about 2,500 mounted infantry and moved into the New Mexico Territory in early January 1862 to confront Federal troops commanded by Col. Edward R. S. Canby.

Canby's 3,800 men occupied Fort Craig, an outpost between Albuquerque and El Paso. Sibley's little army bypassed the Union stronghold and moved north. When Canby ventured out to challenge the Confederates, he met a resounding defeat at Valverde on February 21 and promptly returned to Fort Craig.

The victorious Confederates continued their trek north, aiming for Albuquerque and Santa Fe, which they occupied by March 5. The Union garrisons fled at Sibley's approach, destroying or removing most of the supplies he hoped to appropriate. Now the Texans looked 60 miles northeast of Santa Fe to Fort Union, where remaining Union forces had taken refuge.

On March 10, however, a column of 900 Coloradans under Denver lawyer John P. Slough arrived at Fort Union, setting the stage for the climactic battle of the campaign. Slough ordered most of the garrison to join him on an offensive against the Confederates at Santa Fe. Their march followed the only practical route: via Glorieta Pass on the Santa Fe Trail. Unknown to Slough, Sibley ordered Lt. Col. William R. Scurry to attack Fort Union by the same route.

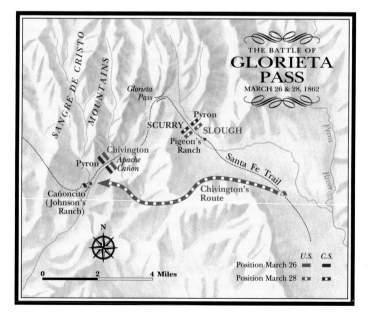

On March 26 the vanguards of the two forces clashed at Apache Canyon, the western end of Glorieta Pass. The surprised Confederates retreated, but when Scurry arrived with reinforcements the next day he decided to renew the advance. Slough also came up on the 27th and developed a brilliant plan. He sent a small flanking party on a circuitous march to the Confederate rear while the main body approached Scurry head-on.

The resulting battle erupted late in the morning of March 28. For six hours Slough and Scurry charged and countercharged, inflicting proportionately high casualties. Near dark the Federals withdrew in apparent defeat. But at 10 p.m. Slough learned that the flanking column had utterly destroyed the Confederate supply train, crippling Sibley's ability to sustain his offensive.

Sibley had no choice but to retreat, finally reaching El Paso in the first week of May. The campaign that culminated at the Battle of Glorieta Pass effectively ended Confederate attempts to secure the West. "The Territory of New Mexico is not worth a quarter of the blood and treasure expended in its conquest," concluded Sibley.

PARK INFORMATION

HEADQUARTERS: Glorieta Unit, Pecos National Historical Park, P. O. Drawer 418, Pecos, NM 87552-0418. Telephone: (505) 757-6414.

DIRECTIONS: No public access to sites as land is still privately owned. Information available by writing superintendent or at Pecos Visitor Center. Two battlefield sites located off I-25: Johnson's Ranch can be seen from exit 293, Pigeon's Ranch can be reached by taking exit 299 to N.M. 50 for 1 mile to marker. To reach Pecos National Historical Park continue on N.M. 50 for 5 miles to town of Pecos. Turn right on N.M. 63; proceed 2 miles south to entrance.

SCHEDULE: Visitor Center open from 8 a.m. to 5 p.m. and from Memorial Day to Labor Day until 6 p.m. Closed Christmas and New Year's Day.

ENTRANCE FEE: $1.00 per person or $3.00 per car.

NEARBY HISTORIC INNS: Bed and Breakfast of New Mexico, P. O. Box 2805, Santa Fe, NM 87504; (505) 982-3332. Statewide reservation service for historic inns.

NORTH CAROLINA

North Carolina offers the paradox of a state that harbored substantial opposition to secession and the Confederacy yet contributed immense resources to the Southern cause. The state gave a majority of its support to moderates in the election of 1860 and narrowly defeated a proposal to call a secession convention in February 1861. Events at Fort Sumter, and Lincoln's subsequent call for troops, drastically altered the political situation. On May 20, 1861, a state convention endorsed separation from the Union and made North Carolina the 11th and final state to join the Confederacy.

North Carolina supplied at least 125,000 soldiers to Confederate armies, a total that exceeded the number of military-age men among the state's 629,942 whites in 1860. More than 40,000 of these men perished in the war, the highest death toll of any Confederate state. Another 3,156 whites enlisted in the Union army, as did 5,035 North Carolina blacks out of an 1860 population in which 331,059 were slaves and 30,463 were free. The roster of 44 Confederate generals born in North Carolina included Braxton Bragg, Leonidas Polk, and William Dorsey Pender. Salisbury Prison held thousands of Union soldiers during the war, earning an unsavory reputation exceeded only by that of Andersonville, Georgia.

▼ *South from Northwest Salient, Fort Fisher*

Governor Zebulon B. Vance guided the state from 1862 to 1865. He opposed interference from the Confederate government in such activities as raising and equipping troops, and he insisted that more North Carolinians should hold important national positions. Frequently seen as a parochial politician who weakened the Confederate war effort, Vance was in reality an excellent wartime leader who supported state relief for families of soldiers, helped keep clothing and food flowing to Confederate forces in Virginia and elsewhere, and encouraged blockade runners to smuggle vital goods past Union patrols to North Carolina harbors. As the war progressed, Vance faced his constituents' increasing disaffection with the Confederacy. Long before the end of the conflict the western regions of North Carolina harbored thousands of deserters and draft evaders who preyed on civilians and resisted both state and national authority.

More than 310 military actions took place in North Carolina, many of them along the coast. Roanoke Island and New Bern fell to an expedition under Union Brig. Gen. Ambrose E. Burnside in the spring of 1862. Wilmington, a haven for blockade runners defended by Fort Fisher, served as the target of repeated Northern efforts. Combined Union forces, which included a fleet boasting the most firepower a navy had ever amassed, reduced Fort Fisher on January 13–15, 1865, and Wilmington capitulated five weeks later. Sherman's army entered the state in March 1865, capturing Fayetteville on the 11th and winning a victory at Averasboro on the 16th. The largest land battle in the state took place on March 19–21 at Bentonville, where Sherman defeated a motley force under Gen. Joseph E. Johnston. On April 26, 1865, Johnston surrendered his army to Sherman near Chapel Hill, bringing the war in North Carolina to an end.

National Historic Landmark

■ FORT FISHER
For information, contact:
P. O. Box 68
Kure Beach, NC 28449
(919) 458-5538
Located 18 miles south of
Wilmington on US 421.

OHIO

O hio played a pivotal role in securing Union victory despite its numerous Democrats, many of whom opposed the policies of the Lincoln administration. After supporting Lincoln for President, the state mobilized enormous resources in the wake of the firing on Fort Sumter. A count of 2,303,374 whites and 36,225 free blacks in 1860 made Ohio the third most populous state in the nation. It also stood third in men contributed to the Union cause with 304,814 white and 5,092 black soldiers, 35,475 of whom lost their lives. An agricultural giant, Ohio ranked high as a grower of wheat and corn and led the nation in wool production. Manufacturing strengths included flour mills and petroleum refineries. Ohio's 2,900-mile railroad network topped that of any other state, and Lake Erie and the Ohio River provided additional ways to transport goods. Without Ohio's men and materials, the progress of Northern arms would have slowed considerably.

Political and military leaders from Ohio figured prominently in Union affairs. Edwin M. Stanton skillfully directed the War Department from 1862 through 1865, while Salmon P. Chase ran the Treasury until he was appointed Chief Justice of the United States in 1864. Radical Republican Benjamin F. Wade and moderate John Sherman wielded great influence in the Senate. From his seat in the House of Representatives, Democrat Samuel S. "Sunset" Cox vociferously attacked Republicans for undermining the Constitution in their zeal to defeat the Confederacy. Fifty-seven generals born in Ohio led Union troops, among them Ulysses S. Grant, William T. Sherman (the senator's older brother), William S. Rosecrans, George A. Custer, and future Presidents James A. Garfield and Rutherford B. Hayes.

Wartime political tensions in Ohio reached their apogee during Clement L. Vallandigham's campaign for the governorship in 1863. The nation's leading anti-war Democrat, Vallandigham called for an immediate armistice, repudiation of the Emancipation Proclamation, and removal of "King Lincoln." Vallandigham threatened Union morale because he had become a rallying figure for Copperheads (anti-war Democrats) across the North. Arrested

Confederate monument, Johnson's Island

on grounds that his statements constituted treason, he was exiled to the Confederacy and eventually made his way to Canada.

Scarcely any military engagements occurred on Ohio soil. The one notable exception was Brig. Gen. John Hunt Morgan's cavalry raid across the Ohio River in July 1863. Hoping to inspire an uprising among Copperheads, Morgan rode through southern Indiana and Ohio, skirmishing with local troops and diverting thousands of soldiers from other tasks. Morgan covered hundreds of miles before being captured near West Point, Ohio, on July 26. Confined in the state penitentiary, he subsequently escaped and resumed his military career.

Few Confederates escaped Johnson's Island, a prison camp located in Sandusky Bay on Lake Erie. First occupied by 500 or 600 prisoners in February 1862, the camp, which received a number of generals and a high percentage of other officers, held some 3,000 Confederates at the end of the war.

National Historic Landmark

■ JOHNSON'S ISLAND
For information, write:
Baycliffs Corp.
15400 Pearl Road, #234
Strongsville, OH 44136
Cemetery open to public, located off Bayshore Road near Marblehead. Prison and fort sites under excavation; special tours can be arranged with site archaeologist.

PENNSYLVANIA

Pennsylvania lived up to its nickname, the Keystone State, through stalwart contributions to Union victory. The state voted Republican in the presidential election of 1860 and was the first to answer Lincoln's call for volunteers in April 1861. Home to 2,849,997 whites and 56,373 free blacks in 1860, Pennsylvania contributed 315,017 white and 8,612 black soldiers to Union armies. It ranked second to New York both in total population and men in service and loomed equally large in industrial might. Pennsylvania led the nation in production of coal, accounted for one-half of all pig iron, and experienced booming growth in the emerging petroleum industry. Nearly 2,500 miles of Pennsylvania railroads linked western states to the Northeast, carrying vast quantities of goods and expediting troop movements. The largest training center in the North was at Camp Curtin in Harrisburg, where more than 300,000 Union soldiers prepared for war.

Sixty-two Union generals were born in Pennsylvania, including such key figures as George Gordon Meade, Winfield Scott Hancock, John F. Reynolds, and Herman Haupt. Josiah Gorgas, the Confederate ordnance wizard, and John C. Pemberton, the commanding general at Vicksburg in 1862–63, also hailed from Pennsylvania. On the political side, Thaddeus Stevens influenced congressional handling of emancipation and other issues as a member of the House, while Simon Cameron, a state Republican boss, became known for his corrupt practices as Secretary of War during the first year of the conflict.

Cameron's bitter rival in Pennsylvania was Andrew Gregg Curtin, the Republican governor. A tireless supporter of the Union, Curtin pressed industrialists to increase war-related production, worked hard for the relief of soldiers' families, and saw that Pennsylvania contributed at least its share of manpower. Curtin convened a meeting of Northern governors at Altoona on September 24, 1862, to affirm support for Lincoln's policies. All but one of

Little Round Top and Valley of Death, Gettysburg

the executives signed a strong statement, though in doing so they risked political opposition at home. Known as "the soldiers' friend," Curtin was less popular with labor. Opposition to the draft and unhappiness with working conditions created a volatile situation in the anthracite coal regions and elsewhere, and Curtin's use of troops to enforce conscription and suppress strikes embittered many workers.

Pennsylvania witnessed more military action than any other Northern state. Confederate cavalry under Maj. Gen. J. E. B. Stuart raided Chambersburg in early October 1862. Brig. Gen. John McCausland's horsemen paid a more destructive visit to that city in July 1864. Acting on orders from Lt. Gen. Jubal A. Early, McCausland burned two-thirds of Chambersburg on July 30 when local leaders refused to pay a ransom. The largest battle of the entire war was fought at Gettysburg on July 1–3, 1863, between Meade's Army of the Potomac and Lee's Army of Northern Virginia. Meade's victory compelled Lee to leave Pennsylvania. It also inspired Lincoln's remarkable address at the dedication of a national cemetery at Gettysburg on November 19, 1863, in which the President brilliantly captured the enduring meaning of the war.

GETTYSBURG

The Battle of Gettysburg, fought on the first three days of July 1863, is the best-known military engagement in American history. More has been written about Gettysburg than about any other Civil War topic, and visitors tour the much-monumented Pennsylvania battlefield in huge numbers each year. While not all historians agree that Gettysburg marked the high tide of the Confederacy, this Northern victory unquestionably represented an important turning point in the war.

Gen. Robert E. Lee and his Army of Northern Virginia assumed the initiative during the Gettysburg campaign. Weighing his options after Chancellorsville in May 1863, Lee saw only two alternatives. The Confederates could "either…retire to Richmond and stand a siege, which must ultimately…end in surrender, or…invade Pennsylvania." Military success north of the Potomac might encourage the vocal Northern peace movement, entice England to intervene on behalf of the South, and relieve pressure on Vicksburg and Tennessee by forcing the Federals to detach troops from those distant theaters. At the very least Lee could feed his hungry soldiers on the rich pro-duce of the Cumberland Valley while providing Virginia's farmers an opportunity to plant and tend their crops.

Furthermore Lee had complete confidence in his army, now organized into three corps of infantry commanded by Lt. Gens. James Longstreet, Richard S. Ewell, and A. P. Hill. Counting artillery and a reinforced cavalry division under Maj. Gen. J. E. B. Stuart, Lee led a force of nearly 80,000 men.

Ewell's corps began moving northwest from its positions near Fredericksburg, Virginia, on June 3. Maj. Gen. Joseph Hooker, at the head of the Army of the Potomac, learned of the Confederate movement and sent his cavalry to determine its extent and meaning. On June 9 the Federal troopers encountered Stuart's brigades at Brandy Station, near Culpeper. The battle, the largest cavalry clash of the war, had little direct influence on Lee's plans. But it marked the first time Union horsemen fought as skilfully as their vaunted opponents.

Ewell continued his march north, crossed the Blue Ridge Mountains, and gobbled up the enemy garrison at Winchester. On June 15 the first Confederates splashed across the Potomac, and

BATTLE FACTS

Battle dates	July 1–3, 1863
Combat strength	U.S. 83,300; C.S. 75,100
Casualties	U.S. 23,000; C.S. 28,100
Commanders	U.S. Maj. Gen. George G. Meade C.S. Gen. Robert E. Lee

by June 24 most of Lee's army was in Maryland or Pennsylvania. Hooker also shifted north, keeping between Lee and Washington. His cavalry sparred with Stuart east of the mountains as the Confederate troopers protected Lee's invasion and supply route through the Shenandoah Valley. On June 24 Stuart received conditional permission from Lee to execute a raid around Hooker's army, provided the Federals remained south of the Potomac. Stuart departed on one of his spectacular rides, but this time his exploits would do more harm than good. He would not rejoin Lee until July 2.

While Stuart's cavalry galloped around the rear of their baffled Union counterparts, Hooker concentrated his 90,000 men near Frederick, Maryland. Fighting Joe's failure at Chancellorsville had made his removal likely, but the administration needed an excuse to act. When Hooker tendered his resignation on June 27 as a ploy to win a dispute with his Washington superiors, Lincoln quickly accepted it. The President

named the 47-year-old chief of the Fifth Corps, Maj. Gen. George G. Meade, as the new army commander.

Meade reluctantly accepted his new post. The new commander possessed an irascible temper and solid professional credentials, and enjoyed the respect, if not the affection, of his subordinates. His goal would be to protect Washington and force Lee to fight before the Confederates reached the Susquehanna River in Pennsylvania. Some of Ewell's corps had already seen the banks of that stream, but when a Confederate spy reported the proximity of Meade's army, the startled Lee, . deprived of Stuart's reliable scouting, ordered his scattered divisions to concentrate east of South Mountain near Cashtown.

Neither Meade nor Lee intended to fight at Gettysburg. But a glance at the map marked the town of 2,500 for attention: ten roads from all points of the compass converged there. Union cavalry under Brig. Gen. John Buford occupied the town on June 30 to

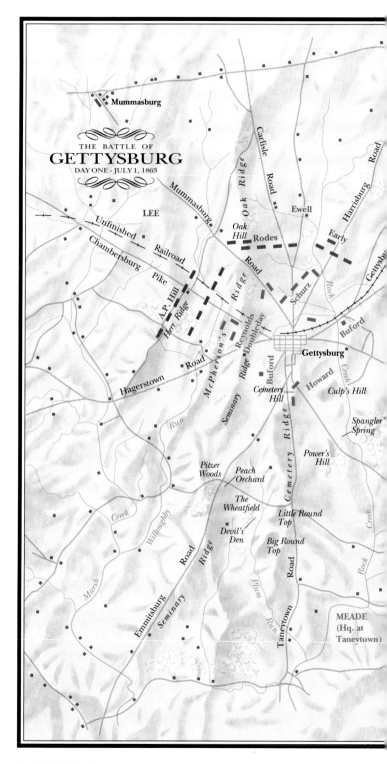

THE BATTLE OF
GETTYSBURG
DAY ONE · JULY 1, 1863

Mummasburg

Carlisle Road

Harrisburg Road

Oak Ridge

LEE

Mummasburg Road

Ewell

Oak Hill

Rodes

Early

Unfinished

Railroad

Chambersburg Pike

Oak Ridge Road

Schurz

Rock

Gettysb

A. P. Hill

Herr Ridge

Ridge

Reynolds

Doubleday

Buford

Hagerstown

McPherson's Ridge

Road

Seminary Ridge

Buford

Gettysburg

Howard

Culp's Hill

Cemetery Hill

Run

Spangler' Spring

Cemetery Ridge

Power's Hill

Pitzer Woods

Peach Orchard

The Wheatfield

Little Round Top

Creek

Devil's Den

Big Round Top

Willoughby

Emmitsburg Road

Seminary Ridge

Plum Run

Taneytown Road

Rock

Marsh

MEADE
(Hq. at Taneytown)

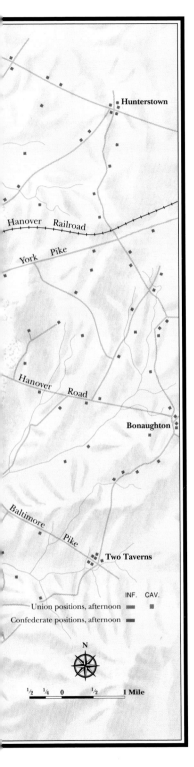

Hunterstown

Hanover   Railroad

York   Pike

Hanover   Road

Bonaughton

Baltimore

Pike

Two Taverns

INF.   CAV.

Union positions, afternoon

Confederate positions, afternoon

N

½ ¼ 0   ½   1 Mile

secure that hub. The following morning two Confederate divisions approached Gettysburg from the west in search of a reported supply of shoes. The resulting meeting would escalate into the worst bloodletting ever witnessed in North America.

Buford's cavalry, using their rapid-firing carbines, held their own against three times their number until Union infantry under Maj. Gen. John F. Reynolds appeared from the south. As Reynolds helped deploy the famous Iron Brigade, a Confederate marksman shot him behind the right ear. Despite Reynolds's death the Federals counterattacked with a vengeance south of the Chambersburg Pike, driving back the Confederates and capturing Brig. Gen James J. Archer. North of the road, part of a Mississippi and North Carolina brigade surrendered en masse in the deep cut of an unfinished railroad.

A lull now descended on the battlefield as reinforcements rushed to the scene. The Union Eleventh Corps took position north of Gettysburg in a thin line while two divisions of Ewell's corps appeared opposite them. In mid-afternoon Ewell's men renewed the offensive. They met stiff resistance from Reynolds's troops, but a division of the Eleventh Corps that had been unwisely posted on a little knoll broke after a short struggle. When Lee at last accepted the battle his subordinates had started and committed fresh troops to test the Federals again along the Chambersburg Pike, the entire Union line collapsed. Northern fugitives sought safety on a prepared position south of town called Cemetery Hill. Aided by the calming influence of Maj. Gen.

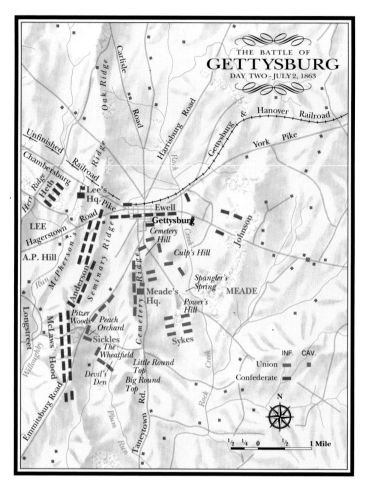

THE BATTLE OF
GETTYSBURG
DAY TWO · JULY 2, 1863

Carlisle Road

Oak Ridge

Harrisburg Road

Rock

Gettysburg & Hanover Railroad

York Pike

Unfinished Railroad

Chambersburg Ridge

Herr Ridge

Heth

Lee's Hq.

Pike

Ewell

Gettysburg

Johnson

LEE

Hagerstown Road

A.P. Hill

McPherson's

Anderson

Seminary Ridge

Cemetery Hill

Culp's Hill

Spangler's Spring

MEADE

Run

Meade's Hq.

Power's Hill

Longstreet

McLaws

Hood

Pitzer Woods

Peach Orchard

Sickles

The Wheatfield

Cemetery Ridge

Sykes

Willoughby

Devil's Den

Little Round Top

Big Round Top

Run

Emmitsburg Road

Taneytown Rd.

Plum

Run

Rock Creek

INF. CAV.

Union

Confederate

N

½ ¼ 0 ½ 1 Mile

Winfield S. Hancock, the Federals rallied. Lee authorized Ewell to assault the new Union stronghold if he thought it "practicable," but Ewell declined. The first day's battle had ended, although new units from both armies poured onto the field after dark.

General Longstreet pressed Lee to assume the tactical defensive: that is, to adopt a strong position between Meade and the city of Washington and force the Federals to attack. Whether this idea was feasible or not, Lee quickly rejected it. The Army of Northern Virginia would attack,

as it had done so successfully at Chancellorsville.

Meade's line on the morning of July 2 took the shape of a fishhook. The barb rested on a rocky prominence called Culp's Hill, the bend in the hook encompassed Cemetery Hill, and the shank ran south down Cemetery Ridge, ending at two knobs called Big and Little Round Top. Lee first hoped to capture Culp's Hill, but when Ewell told him he could not do so, the Confederate commander decided to assault the southern end of the Union line. Longstreet would bear responsibil-

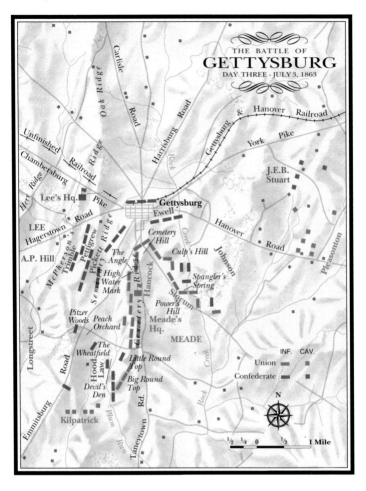

THE BATTLE OF
GETTYSBURG
DAY THREE · JULY 3, 1863

ity for this offensive, a job he was loath to accept. Lee's most experienced corps commander pouted and delayed. Not until 4 p.m. was Longstreet ready to go forward.

Once the Confederates stepped out, however, they displayed the prowess that had earned them so much renown. Maj. Gen. John B. Hood's division struck first, improvising an attack against the Round Tops. Improvisation was required because the Union Third Corps under Maj. Gen. Daniel Sickles had advanced without orders to a position west of Cemetery Ridge and the Round Tops. Sickles

hinged his line on the high ground of the Peach Orchard, deploying one division southeast to a jumble of huge boulders known as Devil's Den and the other northeast along the Emmitsburg Road. Hood saw that the unoccupied Round Tops held the key to the entire Union line, and he aimed to control them.

Hood fell wounded early in the action, but his men quickly seized the wooded Big Round Top and headed north for the open slopes of Little Round Top. Brig. Gen. Gouverneur K. Warren, the chief topographical engineer of the

Army of the Potomac, had recognized the critical importance of Little Round Top. He rushed troops to its crest just in time to repulse the Confederates.

Meanwhile the rest of Longstreet's men stormed into the Peach Orchard, overrunning Sickles's outgunned defenders. The combat swirled through the Wheat Field east of the Peach Orchard as Meade hurried reinforcements to the threatened line. The Wheat Field changed hands half a dozen times while additional Confederate brigades from Hill's corps approached Cemetery Ridge farther north. Eighty-two percent of the 1st Minnesota Infantry fell wounded or dead during a desperate counterattack that helped save Cemetery Ridge by the narrowest of margins. Near nightfall Ewell

◼ *8th Pennsylvania Cavalry Monument, Gettysburg*

attacked Culp's and Cemetery Hills, but these brave actions also fell barely short of success.

That night at a Union council of war Meade and his corps commanders elected "to stay and fight it out," in Maj. Gen. Henry W. Slocum's words. The next morning, over Longstreet's violent objections, Lee decided to attack again, this time against the Union center. The battle on July 3 began at Culp's Hill. There, during a fierce five-hour contest, the Federals forced Ewell out of the trenches he had captured the previous evening. Lee now pinned his hopes on a massive frontal attack using 11 infantry brigades, including the fresh Virginia division of Maj. Gen. George E. Pickett.

The Confederates preceded their assault with a huge artillery bombardment, the heaviest in the war so far. Some 150 guns shelled Cemetery Ridge for nearly two

hours. But most of their shots fell long while the Union batteries slowed their fire to save ammunition for the infantry attack they knew must follow.

The Confederate line stepped out at 3 p.m. With ranks dressed perfectly and banners flying in the breeze, 12,000 Southern men marched into immortality. The action, misnamed Pickett's Charge (Pickett commanded less than half the troops), carried the Confederates toward a copse of chestnut oaks near an angle in a stone wall. Only a handful of Southerners reached their goal, and half never returned to their lines. As the survivors poured back to the starting point on Seminary Ridge, Lee greeted them. "This was all my fault," he said. "It is I that have lost this fight, and you must help me out of it the best way you can."

Lee began his retreat on the night of July 4. Meade did not follow up his victory of July 3, nor did he pursue Lee with vigor when the Confederates slipped away. Ten days later, to Lincoln's dismay, the Army of Northern Virginia had recrossed the Potomac virtually unmolested.

The butcher's bill at Gettysburg was staggering. Lee lost 28,100 men, more than one-third of his army. The Federals suffered 23,000 casualties, reflecting their defensive posture throughout the battle. Despite the dimensions of this defeat, Gettysburg did not cripple the Army of Northern Virginia; Lee would remain in the field another 21 months. But combined with the capture of Vicksburg, Meade's victory in Pennsylvania gave citizens in the North reason to believe that the Union would be restored.

PARK INFORMATION

HEADQUARTERS: Gettysburg National Military Park, P. O. Box 1080, Gettysburg, PA 17325-1080. Telephone: (717) 334-1124.

DIRECTIONS: Located 37 miles southwest of Harrisburg on US 15 (business) in city of Gettysburg.

SCHEDULE: Park roads open daily from 6 a.m. to 10 p.m. Visitor facilities open daily from 8 a.m. to 5 p.m. Closed Thanksgiving, Christmas, and New Year's Day.

FEES: Ages 16–62, $2.00 for Electric Map program and $2 for Cyclorama. Over 62, $1.50. Groups $1.50 per adult. Guides may be hired for two-hour or longer battlefield tours ($20 per car, $50 per bus). Bus groups should send written reservation requests.

TOURS: Park can be toured by car, bike, foot, or horseback. Four hiking trails. Self-guided auto tour beginning at Visitor Center follows 18-mile route past 16 tour stops with explanatory markers.

POINTS OF INTEREST:
■ **Visitor Center** Houses Rosensteel Collection of Civil War artifacts, Electric Map program, and Cyclorama Center.
■ **Gettysburg National Cemetery** Marker 16. Scene of Lincoln's Gettysburg Address.

NEARBY HISTORIC INNS: Amanda's Regional Reservation Service for Bed and Breakfast, 1428 Park Ave., Baltimore, MD 21217; (410) 225-0001. Statewide reservation service for historic inns. Gettysburg, Harpers Ferry, Antietam, and Monocacy battlefields are close to each other. Inns listed for one battlefield may be convenient to others.

SOUTH CAROLINA

I t is difficult to imagine the outbreak of the American Civil War without the influence of South Carolina. Many Northerners took this view, as evidenced by Sherman's observation in December 1864 that his army was "burning with an insatiable desire to wreak vengeance upon South Carolina. I almost tremble at her fate, but feel that she deserves all that seems in store for her." Between 1830 and 1860 South Carolinians championed first nullification and then secession. Many cheered Representative Preston Brooks in 1856 when he caned Senator Charles Sumner, a leading abolitionist, on the floor of the Senate. They responded to Lincoln's election by seceding on December 20, 1860, and war engulfed the nation after Southern batteries in Charleston Harbor fired on Fort Sumter on April 12, 1861. South Carolina had led the way toward separation and bloodshed, pulling ten other states along a tragic road.

In 1860 South Carolina's population stood at 291,300 whites and 412,408 blacks (of whom 10,002 were free). Only remote Florida among Southern states had fewer whites, yet South Carolina sent between 60,000 and 70,000 men into the Confederate army. Some 13,000 died in uniform, nearly one-quarter of the 1860 military-age pool of 55,000. The state furnished no white troops to the Union, though 5,462 of its black men served in Federal units. Forty-eight natives of South Carolina became Confederate generals, including Wade Hampton, Stephen D. Lee, and Joseph B. Kershaw.

Of 224 living graduates of the South Carolina Military Academy (The Citadel), 209 served in the Confederate armies, and Christopher G. Memminger was Jefferson Davis's Secretary of the Treasury.

Military actions in South Carolina, which totaled some 240 encounters, wrought only minor damage until late in the war. Much early activity involved Federal operations against coastal targets. On November 8, 1861, Union naval and land forces took control of the area around Port Royal, which soon became a major base for blockade vessels patrolling the south Atlantic

coast. The nearby Sea Islands also witnessed the North's earliest Reconstruction program. Here government agencies and Northern civilians worked to ease the transition of local blacks from slavery to freedom while trying to maintain the production of long-staple cotton. The port of Charleston, guarded by Fort Sumter, saw its commerce choked off by blockaders but resisted capture until the Rebels evacuated in February 1865.

Sherman's soldiers brought the war home to South Carolina's interior. Entering the state on February 1, 1865, they inflicted far greater property damage than they

▲ *Fort Sumter*

had during their more celebrated march from Atlanta to Savannah. On February 17 the Federals took possession of Columbia, most of which burned in raging fires that night. South Carolinians spoke of Sherman's atrocities in Columbia, but at least some of the fires were set by retreating Confederates seeking to destroy supplies of cotton. Sherman's armies left widespread ruin behind as they moved on to North Carolina in March. South Carolina, the Cradle of Secession, had paid a fearful price for its experiment in rebellion.

FORT SUMTER

No Southern city embraced secession with more passion than Charleston, South Carolina. A convention gathered there in December 1860 and voted unanimously to take the Palmetto State out of the Union. Militia units quickly rushed to Charleston, eager to defend South Carolina's independence. The only visible enemy, however, was a tiny garrison of U.S. troops who occupied Fort Moultrie on the north side of the harbor.

Maj. Robert Anderson commanded Fort Moultrie and the two other installations that guarded Charleston Harbor. A Southerner by birth and marriage, Anderson was also a career officer whose loyalty to his service was unflinch-

ing. On the night of December 26 he loaded his men into boats and evacuated his vulnerable post in favor of Fort Sumter, a pentagonal fort on an artificial island 3.3 miles from Charleston beside the main ship channel. This brick bastion offered Anderson security from land attack and protection from long-range artillery. But although the fort had been under construction for more than 30 years, only 75 of the prescribed 135 guns were in casemates or on the ramparts by April 1861. Moreover, Anderson's force numbered but 85 officers and men, assisted by 43 civilian laborers.

Fort Sumter instantly became a symbol of sovereignty to both Northerners and South Carolin-

BATTLE FACTS

Battle dates	April 12–14, 1861
Combat strength	U.S. 85; C.S. 5,000
Casualties	U.S. 85 (83 paroled); C.S. 4
Commanders	U.S. Maj. Robert Anderson C.S. Brig. Gen. P. G. T. Beauregard

ians. President James Buchanan, vacillating and hoping to postpone a showdown until his term expired, at last decided to reinforce Anderson secretly via the unarmed merchant ship *Star of the West*. News of the scheme reached Charleston, and on January 9, 1861, South Carolina cannoneers turned back

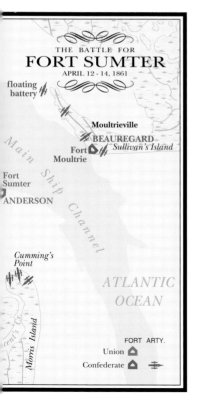

THE BATTLE FOR
FORT SUMTER
APRIL 12 - 14, 1861

floating battery

Moultrieville

BEAUREGARD
Fort
Moultrie *Sullivan's Island*

Fort Sumter
ANDERSON

Main Ship Channel

Cumming's Point

ATLANTIC OCEAN

Morris Island

FORT ARTY.
Union
Confederate

the attempt. This act of aggression or self-defense, depending on the sectional viewpoint, ignited a flurry of angry editorials. Within a few weeks six states had followed South Carolina out of the Union.

Meanwhile the fort's supplies continued to dwindle. On March 5, the day after Abraham Lincoln's inauguration, word arrived in Washington that the garrison needed help. Anderson reported that Confederate forces had heavily fortified the harbor and that he lacked enough food, ammunition, and manpower to meet the threat. Lincoln sent agents to Charleston to see whether an expedition could land at Fort Sumter. At the same time Secretary of State William Seward took it upon himself to assure South Carolinians that Sumter would be abandoned.

Seward's unauthorized diplomacy backfired. Lincoln opted to hold Fort Sumter and on March 29 began to outfit a relief mission designed to provide only food, not reinforcements or munitions, to Anderson's beleaguered command. Lincoln informed the governor of South Carolina of his intentions, placing the Confederates in an awkward position. If the Southerners wanted Sumter, they had to initiate war for the immediate purpose of denying sustenance to hungry men. Yet they also felt betrayed by Seward's empty promises. Why should they believe the administration now when it had already proven perfidious?

The military commander at Charleston, Brig. Gen. P. G. T. Beauregard, had assembled 5,000 impatient soldiers and ringed Fort Sumter with batteries. As the bloodless crisis entered its third month, pressure mounted for a resolution. Beauregard and the new Confederate administration in Montgomery, Alabama, worried that a continued stalemate would weaken their ability to control the armed amateurs around Charleston. On April 10 Secretary of War Leroy P. Walker instructed Beauregard to demand Sumter's immediate evacuation and, if Anderson refused, to "proceed, in such manner as you may determine, to reduce it."

The next day a three-man delegation appeared at Sumter with Walker's ultimatum. Anderson declined to capitulate but hinted that he would be forced to quit the fort in a few days when his supplies ran out. The Confederate commissioners reported this to Beauregard, who wired Montgomery for instructions. Walker permitted the general to withhold fire pending a commitment from Anderson to leave the fort.

The messengers returned to Sumter after midnight with the new conditions. Major Anderson consulted with his officers (five of whom would go on to become generals in the Union army) and replied that he would evacuate the fort on April 15 unless he was fired upon or received supplies or new orders from his government.

Col. James Chesnut, an aide to Beauregard, found this answer too equivocal and told Anderson, "we have the honor to notify you that [Beauregard] will open the fire of his batteries on Fort Sumter in one hour." The gauntlet had at last been dropped.

At 4:30 a.m. on April 12, 1861, Lt. Henry S. Farley sent a shell arching over the dark waters around Fort Sumter, the signal to commence the bombardment. "Shot and shell went screaming over Sumter as if an army of devils were swooping around it," remembered a witness. Capt. Abner Doubleday, Anderson's senior officer, fired the first answering shot about 7 a.m., but the contest proved a mismatch from the start. Anderson could safely employ only the 21 guns protected in masonry casemates. Because he had no fuses, he used only solid shot. A shortage of powder bags for cartridges kept the garrison busy improvising substitutes and prompted Anderson to reduce his rate of fire.

Beauregard suffered no such handicaps, and his gunners soon found Sumter's range. Heated projectiles set the fort's buildings ablaze, choking the garrison with smoke and imperiling the powder magazines. At the end of the day, one of Anderson's officers reported, the fort "presented a picture of havoc and ruin."

Anderson hoped to hold on long enough for relief ships to reach him, but high seas and Confederate fire kept them from doing so. The barrage resumed on April 13 with equal fury, and Anderson recognized that the end was near. When a cannonball tore away Sumter's flagstaff, a former Texas senator named Louis T. Wigfall thought the time had arrived for negotiations. Without Beauregard's approval, Wigfall brazenly rowed to the fort and met with Anderson, who found his terms acceptable. At 1:30 p.m. the Federals raised a white flag.

Shortly after Wigfall's departure Beauregard's real spokesmen arrived and informed the outraged Union commander that his surrender was invalid. For a moment it seemed as if the battle would resume; then Beauregard endorsed Wigfall's provisions, and at 7 p.m. Anderson officially capitulated.

Nearly 3,400 missiles rained on Fort Sumter during the 34-hour cannonade, but only four of the fort's defenders had been wounded—by flying bricks. Confederate casualties were equally insignificant. The only fatalities occurred during Anderson's 100-gun salute on April 14 when a charge exploded prematurely, killing Pvt. Daniel Hough and mortally wounding another Union soldier. Anderson canceled the rest of the ceremony, and his men boarded a steamer to be ferried to the Union fleet for transport home.

Confederate forces immediately occupied Fort Sumter. During the next three years, they repulsed several determined attempts to recapture it. Sumter's critical location at the entrance to Charleston Harbor kept the Union navy from attacking the city and enabled the garrison to receive supplies and ammunition from shore. The Federal army secured positions from which they pummeled the fort with artillery, reducing its masonry to rubble. Still, the sand and bricks sufficiently protected Sumter's defenders from amphibious assault. Not until Sherman's army approached Charleston over land in February 1865 did the city become defenseless. Ruined, defiant, and at last abandoned, Fort Sumter mirrored failed Southern hopes for independence.

PARK INFORMATION

HEADQUARTERS: Fort Sumter National Monument, 1214 Middle St., Sullivan's Island, SC 29482. Telephone: (803) 883-3123.

DIRECTIONS: Accessible only by boat. Tour boats leave from City Marina and Patriots Point for 2 1/4-hour tour. City Marina is on Lockwood Drive, just south of US 17 in Charleston. To reach Patriots Point take US 17 north from Charleston and follow signs. Free parking at both locations. For boat schedules call (803) 722-1691 or write Fort Sumter Tours, Inc., P. O. Box 59, Charleston, SC 29402.

SCHEDULE: Open daily from 9 a.m. to 6 p.m. June 15 to Labor Day. Hours vary rest of year. Closed Christmas.

FEES: Boat tour $8.00 for adults, $4.00 under 12 years, and free under 6 years. Tickets may be purchased at dock. Group rates available; reservations recommended.

TOURS: Rangers provide interpretive services. Museum located at fort.

POINT OF INTEREST: **Fort Moultrie** Interpretive exhibits within fort and Visitor Center.

NEARBY HISTORIC INNS: Historic Charleston Bed & Breakfast, 43 Legare St., Charleston, SC 29402; (803) 722-6606. Statewide reservation service for historic inns.

TENNESSEE

T ennessee seceded reluctantly, only to become one of the war's major battle-grounds. Its electoral votes in 1860 went to Senator John Bell, a native son who ran as the Unionist candidate. On February 9, 1861, Tennesseans voted 68,282 to 59,449 against holding a secession convention. But Lincoln's call for troops after Fort Sumter triggered a change of mood. Governor Isham G. Harris condemned Lincoln's "bloody and tyrannical policy," and the state legislature approved a military league with the Confederacy on May 7. One month later, on June 8, Tennessee's voters endorsed secession 104,913 to 47,238.

▼ *Confederate artillery emplacement, Lookout Mountain*

Sentiment against the Confederacy remained strong in mountainous east Tennessee. Andrew Johnson continued to occupy his seat in the United States Senate, the only Southern senator to do so, while William G. "Parson" Brownlow, editor of the Knoxville *Whig*, promised to "fight the Secession leaders till Hell freezes over, and then fight them on the ice." The Confederate government never completely controlled the region.

The second most populous Confederate state, Tennessee was home to 826,782 whites, 275,719 black slaves, and 7,300 free blacks in 1860. It contributed 31,092 white and 20,133 black soldiers to the Union, of whom 8,777 whites and an undetermined number of blacks lost their lives.

The Confederate army enrolled approximately 100,000 whites; roughly a quarter did not survive the war. Fifty Confederate and six Union generals were born in Tennessee, including controversial Southern cavalryman Nathan Bedford Forrest.

Tennessee held immense strategic importance for the Confederacy. It led the new nation in producing mules and pork and supplied more horses, corn, and wheat than any other Confederate state east of the Mississippi. Memphis, Nashville, and Chattanooga served as centers of manufacturing, communications, and trade. Four major routes into the Confederacy passed through or bordered on Tennessee—the Mississippi, Cumberland, and Tennessee Rivers and the Louisville & Nashville Railroad.

With more than 1,450 military encounters on its soil, Tennessee ranked second only to Virginia. Grant's victories at Forts Henry and Donelson in February 1862 forced Confederates to evacuate Nashville and were followed shortly by his bloody triumph at Shiloh on April 6–7. Nashville became the headquarters of Lincoln's military government for Tennessee, administered by Andrew Johnson between 1862 and 1864. Gen. Braxton Bragg's Confederate Army of Tennessee fought the inconclusive battle of Stones River (December 31, 1862 & January 2, 1863), and remained in middle Tennessee until Maj. Gen. William S. Rosecrans's Tullahoma Campaign forced a retreat into Georgia in June and July 1863. Bragg pushed Rosecrans back into Chattanooga in September, after which Grant replaced Rosecrans with Maj. Gen. George H. Thomas, breaking an ineffective Confederate siege and winning the Battle of Chattanooga (November 23–25, 1863).

One late Confederate success, Maj. Gen. Nathan Bedford Forrest's capture of Fort Pillow on April 12, 1864, prompted bitter charges that his troopers slaughtered black soldiers who tried to surrender. During Confederate Gen. John Bell Hood's Tennessee Campaign of 1864, his army survived a stinging defeat at Franklin on November 30 only to experience nearly complete disaster in the Battle of Nashville on December 15–16. Hood's subsequent retreat ended major military operations in a state ravaged by four years of constant fighting.

National Historic Landmarks

■ FORT PILLOW
For information, contact:
Route 2, Box 108 B1
Henning, TN 38041
(901) 738-5581
Located 18 miles west of Henning off Tenn. 87.

■ FRANKLIN
Battlefield has been developed. Landmarks consist of Carter House, Carnton Plantation and Confederate Cemetery, Fort Granger, and Winstead Hill.
For information, contact:
Williamson County Chamber of Commerce
City Hall, Suite 107
Franklin, TN 37064
(615) 794-1225
Located 18 miles south of Nashville on I-65.

FORT DONELSON

Confederate military planners recognized the vital importance of protecting the Southern heartland, the region between the Mississippi River and the Appalachian Mountains. By late 1861 Gen. Albert Sidney Johnston had drawn a defensive line from Cumberland Gap on the east to Columbus, Kentucky, on the Mississippi to deflect any Union invasion. Johnston's scheme included two earthen forts blocking major water routes into Dixie. Fort Henry squatted on the east bank of the Tennessee River and Fort Donelson secured the Cumberland River from a plateau only 12 overland miles from Henry. Both strongpoints stood in Tennessee just south of the Kentucky border, having been built while the Bluegrass State indulged in neutrality early in the war.

Union strategists understood that if Forts Henry and Donelson could be conquered, the way to Mississippi and Alabama lay open, nullifying Johnston's cordon to the north. On February 2, 1862, 17,000 Federal soldiers under an obscure brigadier general named Ulysses S. Grant boarded trans-

ports at Cairo, Illinois. A flotilla of gunboats designed for inland waterways and led by Flag Officer Andrew H. Foote accompanied Grant's divisions.

Their first target would be Fort Henry, vulnerable and half submerged in the flood waters of the Tennessee. Most of the Confederate garrison retreated to Fort Donelson before the attack began. On February 6 Foote pummeled the doomed remnant, who surrendered after a short engagement in which Grant's troops played no part.

The fall of Fort Henry prompted Johnston to withdraw from Kentucky and move south through Nashville, Tennessee. Covering his retreat, he dispatched six brigades to hold Fort Donelson until the rest of the Confederate forces crossed the Cumberland River. Then the Donelson contingent would join their comrades farther south.

Johnston erred not only by sending inadequate reinforcements to defend Fort Donelson, but by choosing two of the Confederacy's worst officers to lead them: Brig. Gen. John B. Floyd and Brig. Gen.

BATTLE FACTS

Battle dates	February 12–16, 1862
Combat strength	U.S. 27,000; C.S. 21,000
Casualties	U.S. 2,800; C.S. 13,500
Commanders	U.S. Brig. Gen. Ulysses S. Grant
	Flag Officer Andrew H. Foote
	C.S. Brig. Gen. John B. Floyd
	Brig. Gen. Gideon J. Pillow
	Brig. Gen. Simon B. Buckner

Gideon J. Pillow. Some 15,500 Southern soldiers manned the fort when Grant's army arrived on February 12. The Federals immediately invested the stronghold, although they had too few troops to surround it completely.

A sudden winter storm on February 13 sent the mercury plunging to 10°F, and shivering men on both sides of Donelson's earth-and-log-walls suffered in the cold. The next day four of Foote's gunboats steamed to within 400 yards of Donelson's water batteries and attempted to repeat their accomplishment at Fort Henry. Nine

▲ *National cemetery, Fort Donelson*

heavy guns battered Foote's flotilla, and after sustaining a wound, Foote ordered his captains to drift downstream out of range. "A shout of exultation leaped from the lips of every soldier in the fort," remembered a Confederate. But the situation remained grim. As fresh Union troops arrived, the Southern generals knew they faced a mounting crisis.

Informed that Johnston's army had reached Nashville, Floyd, Pillow, and the third in command, Brig. Gen. Simon B. Buckner, felt justified in abandoning Fort Donelson. They decided to attack the Union right on the morning of the 15th and open the escape route that led south toward the Tennessee capital.

The offensive succeeded brilliantly. By noon the road to Nashville beckoned. The Confederates now had two good options: Withdraw as planned or continue their attacks, building on the momentum achieved in the morning. They did neither. Floyd and Pillow, senselessly worried about Federal advances on the opposite end of the line, ordered their troops back to the fort. Although

Buckner managed to repel Union counterattacks, Grant vigorously repaired the damage wreaked during the Confederate breakout, sealing the graycoats inside Fort Donelson more tightly than before.

That night the Confederate high command concluded that further resistance would be useless. Floyd and Pillow, however, felt unwilling to share the garrison's fate and passed responsibility to Buckner. Before dawn Pillow slipped across the river to safety, and Floyd, taking 3,000 of his Virginia troops with him, escaped upriver on steamers. Col. Nathan Bedford

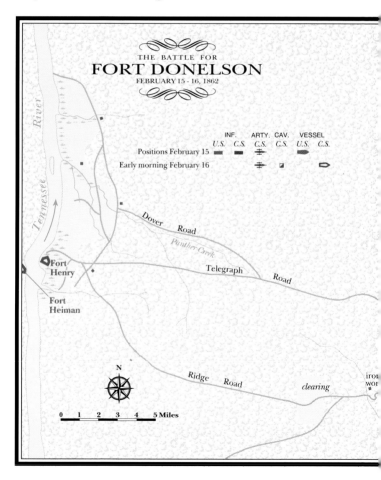

THE BATTLE FOR

FORT DONELSON

FEBRUARY 15 - 16, 1862

Forrest also refused to surrender and led some 700 Confederate cavalry across flooded back roads and into Nashville.

Buckner's request for terms elicited one of the more quoted dispatches of the Civil War. "No terms except unconditional and immediate surrender can be accepted," answered Grant. "I propose to move immediately upon your works." Buckner had no choice but to agree. At least 12,000 Confederate soldiers became prisoners of war, and the North had a new hero: "Unconditional Surrender" Grant.

The fall of Fort Donelson was the first major Union victory of the war. It forced the Confederates out of Kentucky and most of Tennessee and provided the Union an opening wedge toward the ultimate goal in the west: control of the Mississippi River.

PARK INFORMATION

HEADQUARTERS: Fort Donelson National Battlefield, P. O. Box 434, Dover, TN 37058-0434. Telephone: (615) 232-5706.

DIRECTIONS: Located on US 79, 1 mile west of Dover and about 80 miles west of Nashville.

SCHEDULE: Grounds normally open daily during daylight hours. Closed Christmas. Visitor Center open daily from 8 a.m. to 4:30 p.m.

ENTRANCE FEE: None

TOURS: Self-guided auto tour leads past 11 interpretive markers. Visitors can rent or purchase audiotape to accompany tour. Limited special guided tours for school groups in spring.

POINTS OF INTEREST:
■ **Visitor Center** Houses museum of Civil War relics and slide show. ■ **Dover Hotel** (Surrender House) Marker 10. Site of Gen. Simon Buckner's surrender to Gen. Ulysses S. Grant. Restored building serves as park headquarters. ■ **National Cemetery** Marker 11.

NEARBY HISTORIC INNS: Bed and Breakfast Hospitality, P. O. Box 110227, Nashville, TN 37222; (615) 331-5244 or (800) 458-2421 out-of-state. Statewide reservation service for historic inns.

SHILOH

The Union capture of Forts Henry and Donelson in February 1862 forced Confederate Gen. Albert S. Johnston to evacuate most of Tennessee and assume the defensive near Corinth, Mississippi. A vital railroad junction at Corinth connected Memphis and the Mississippi Valley with the eastern Confederacy and the Gulf coast. Aided by his second in command, Gen. P. G. T. Beauregard, Johnston accumulated more than 40,000 troops at Corinth by late March. He divided his Army of the Mississippi into four infantry commands led by Maj. Gens. Leonidas Polk, Braxton Bragg, and William J. Hardee, and Brig. Gen. John C. Breckinridge.

Maj. Gen. Ulysses S. Grant, the North's new military hero follow-ing his victory at Fort Donelson, transported the Army of the Tennessee up its namesake river to Pittsburg Landing in mid-March. He eventually disembarked five infantry divisions (with another just downstream) totaling about 43,000 troops.

Pittsburg Landing provided a convenient jump-off point for a campaign against Corinth, 23 miles to the southwest. Grant, however, had instructions to wait until the Federal army under Maj. Gen. Don Carlos Buell completed its trek from Nashville and joined Grant on the banks of the Tennessee.

Johnston and Beauregard recognized that soon the combined Union armies would greatly outnumber their forces. They planned, therefore, to strike Grant

⊸⊸ BATTLE FACTS ⊸⊸

Battle dates	April 6–7, 1862
Combat strength	U.S. 65,000; C.S. 44,700
Casualties	U.S. 13,000; C.S. 10,700
Commanders	U.S. Maj. Gen. Ulysses S. Grant
	C.S. Gen. Albert S. Johnston (killed)
	Gen. P. G. T. Beauregard

before Buell arrived. Johnston ordered his troops to begin their march on April 3, exhorting them to win "a decisive victory over the agrarian mercenaries sent to subjugate and despoil you of your liberties, property, and honor."

The Southern regiments, despite high motivation, lacked seasoning

and discipline. Rain, the wooded countryside, and inept leadership turned a one-day march into a three-day ordeal. When the grayclad army halted two miles from the Union camps on the afternoon of April 5, Beauregard counseled a countermarch to Corinth. "There is no chance for surprise," he advised Johnston. "Now they will be intrenched to the eyes." Johnston and the two corps commanders disagreed. "I would fight them if they were a million," said Johnston, and the generals plotted their tactics for a dawn assault.

Ignoring numerous reports of the Confederates' proximity, Union leaders discounted the possibility of danger. Brig. Gen. William T. Sherman, in immediate command of the Federal camps, rejected warnings from junior officers, ascribing their anxiety to inexperience or cowardice. On April 5, Grant wired Maj. Gen. Henry W. Halleck in St. Louis that "I have scarcely the faintest idea of an attack being made upon us." To make matters worse, the Northerners deployed with an eye toward comfort rather than defense. The

◀ *Union tent hospital site, Shiloh*

■ *Union battle line near Peach Orchard, Shiloh*

Union army was ripe for disaster.

Johnston's offensive commenced at 5 a.m. April 6. His first objective was the crossroads near Shiloh Church, and the Confederate commander rode forward to direct the attacks personally. Beauregard remained behind to dispatch troops to proper locations on the battlefield.

Hardee's first charge caught Sherman by surprise, and the Federals quickly fell back. Brig.

Gen. Benjamin M. Prentiss's division also met the assault; and supported by the three remaining Union divisions, Yankee resistance stiffened. By 8 a.m. Hardee needed help to maintain his momentum, and Bragg's oversized corps stepped out. Under Bragg's fierce attack, the Union line disintegrated within two hours. Prentiss withdrew a mile to a wooded, sunken road bordered by a rail fence and fronting an open field of fire. The rest of the Federal army extended this new battle line by 10:30 a.m.

In the meantime, Grant arrived at Pittsburg Landing from his headquarters downriver at Savannah. He issued orders to Maj. Gen. Lew Wallace to hasten his division to the battlefield from its camps four miles away. Buell's leading division under Brig. Gen. William Nelson appeared on the east bank, and Grant told the newcomers to march to the river opposite Pittsburg Landing, where transports would ferry them across. As Grant rode ashore, he saw blueclad fugitives crouched under the bluff in abject terror, a grim harbinger for the fate of his army on a day Sherman called "the devil's own."

Union units had not cornered the market on disorganization. Although Confederate morale in victory remained high, command and control evaporated early in the battle. Beauregard discarded his vision of neat assault lines and simply assigned corps commanders to particular segments of the battlefield regardless of whose troops occupied them.

The Southerners' next target would be Prentiss's strongpoint behind the sunken road. Between 12:30 p.m. and 2:30 p.m. four separate attacks unsuccessfully tested this position. A Confederate participant remembered that "they mowed us down at every volley," and another Rebel called the place a "hornets' nest." Some 17,000 Confederates in all would charge the Hornets' Nest, defended by only 4,500 Federals, but at no time did more than 3,700 graycoats assault in unison. "It seemed almost barbarous to fire on brave men pressing forward so heroically to the mouth of hell," thought one Unionist.

While most of the Confederates pounded the Federal center, Johnston led a move around the Union left to cut off the enemy from Pittsburg Landing. A minié ball nicked an artery in his leg and the general's boot filled with blood. When aides discovered the wound, which seemed minor, no one thought to apply a tourniquet. Johnston soon bled to death, and overall command devolved upon Beauregard.

Beauregard continued the unimaginative, piecemeal attacks against the Hornets' Nest despite the vulnerability of the Union flanks. Grant ordered Prentiss to "maintain [his] position at all hazards," and Prentiss obeyed with tenacity. Confederate Brig. Gen. Daniel Ruggles finally broke the impasse by massing 62 cannon opposite the sunken road at 4 p.m. An Iowa officer described the 30-minute bombardment that followed as "a mighty hurricane sweeping everything before it." The Southerners charged again. This time the Union line collapsed. As weary survivors streamed to the

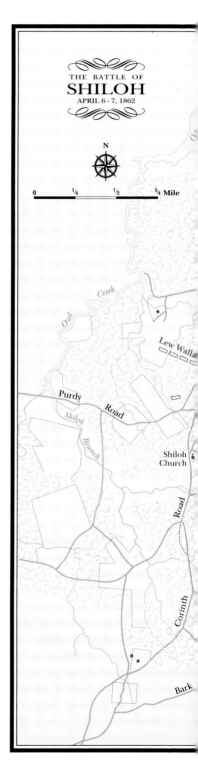

THE BATTLE OF

SHILOH
APRIL 6 - 7, 1862

N

0   ¼   ½   ¾ Mile

Creek

Owl

Lew Walld

Purdy

Road

Shiloh

Branch

Shiloh
Church

Road

Corinth

Bark

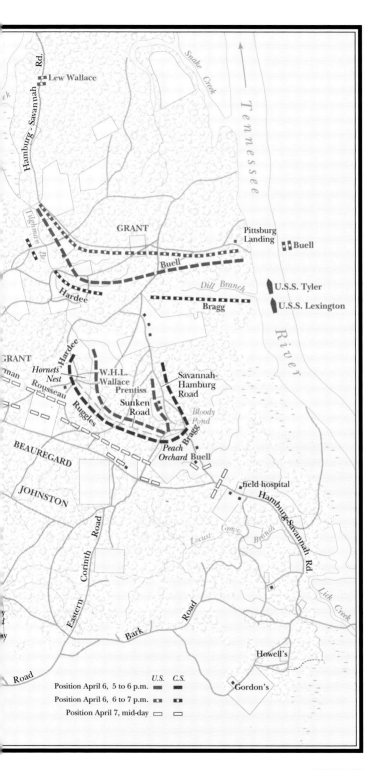

Lew Wallace

Hamburg - Savannah Rd.

Snake Creek

Tennessee

Tighman Br.

GRANT

Pittsburg
Landing

Buell

Buell

Hardee

Dill Branch

Bragg

U.S.S. Tyler

U.S.S. Lexington

River

GRANT

*Hornets'
Nest*

man

Rousseau

Hardee

W.H.L.
Wallace
Prentiss

Savannah-
Hamburg
Road

Ruggles

Sunken
Road

*Bloody
Pond*

BEAUREGARD

Peach
Orchard Buell

Bragg

JOHNSTON

field hospital

Corinth Road

Hamburg-Savannah Rd.

Locust

Grove

Branch

Lick Creek

Eastern

Road

Bark

Road

Howell's

Road

Gordon's

	U.S.	C.S.
Position April 6, 5 to 6 p.m.		
Position April 6, 6 to 7 p.m.		
Position April 7, mid-day		

▲ *Bloody Pond, Shiloh*

rear, one Federal division commander fell mortally wounded in the retreat, but Prentiss remained behind to surrender 2,200 men to the triumphant Confederates.

The Hornets' Nest had held out for seven hours, valuable time used by Grant to fashion a new line closer to the river. Beauregard intended to assault this position at 6 p.m., but canceled his orders at the last minute. His troops were too exhausted and hungry to continue fighting that day. Moreover, the Confederate high command believed that the defeated Grant would use the cover of darkness to escape across the river.

The Southern generals could

not have been more wrong. Grant bolstered his line with fresh troops from Buell and Lew Wallace's tardy division while cold rain fell upon the many wounded from both armies. By daybreak on April 7 Grant had 45,000 men in position, half of them fresh, to challenge 20,000 played-out Confederates.

Grant's counterattack regained the ground lost the previous day. Beauregard rallied his men near Shiloh Church, hoping for the arrival of reinforcements. By 3:30 p.m. he realized no help would be forthcoming. His beaten army then withdrew unmolested, Grant admitting that his troops were too fatigued to pursue. Protecting Beauregard's retreat, Col. Nathan

general's removal followed his tarnished performance at Shiloh. Abraham Lincoln rejected the advice. "I can't spare this man," said the President. "He fights."

Bedford Forrest fought a rearguard cavalry action on April 8 in which he sustained a wound.

Forrest was but one of nearly 24,000 American casualties at Shiloh. Although the Union lost more men, the Confederates suffered a higher proportion of killed, wounded, and captured—some 24 percent. Shiloh was the first large-scale battle of the Civil War, and the magnitude of the carnage shocked civilians both North and South.

Shiloh merely marked a brief interruption in the Union effort to capture Corinth, a goal achieved on May 30 by Grant's superior, General Halleck, after a tortuously slow advance. Halleck was jealous of Grant, and calls for the Illinois

PARK INFORMATION

HEADQUARTERS: Shiloh National Military Park, P. O. Box 67, Shiloh, TN 38376. Telephone: (901) 689-5275.

DIRECTIONS: Located in Shiloh on Tenn. 22, 50 miles south of I-40 and 110 miles east of Memphis via Tenn. 57 or US 64.

SCHEDULE: Visitor Center open daily from 8 a.m. to 5 p.m. and from Memorial Day to Labor Day until 6 p.m. Closed Christmas.

ENTRANCE FEE: Ages 17–61, $1.00 per person or $3.00 per family. Educational groups admitted free. Annual passes available.

TOURS: Visitors may take self-guided auto tour that follows 9.5-mile route with 15 tour stops. Visitors can rent audiotape from bookstore to accompany tour. Cassette players available. Groups can request talks, tours, and demonstrations by calling (901) 689-5275.

POINTS OF INTEREST: ■ **Visitor Center** Houses museum of Civil War military equipment, bookstore, and 25-minute film shown throughout day. ■ **Shiloh National Cemetery** Located between markers 1 and 15, near Visitor Center.

NEARBY HISTORIC INNS: Bed and Breakfast Hospitality, P. O. Box 110227, Nashville, TN 37222; (615) 331-5244 or (800) 458-2421 out-of-state. Statewide reservation service for historic inns.

STONES RIVER

The Confederate war effort in the west peaked in October 1862. Gen. Braxton Bragg led Southern forces almost to the Ohio River before losing the Battle of Perryville, Kentucky. He then withdrew into Tennessee and concentrated his army at Murfreesboro, 30 miles south of Nashville.

The victorious Federals named Maj. Gen. William S. Rosecrans to head the reorganized Army of the Cumberland. After reinforcing Nashville and transforming the city into a supply and operations base, Rosecrans ordered 44,000 of his men to move south against Bragg. Three infantry corps left Nashville on December 26 and approached Murfreesboro four days later.

As military bands from both sides played patriotic airs, culminating in a spontaneous and emotional joint rendition of "Home Sweet Home," Bragg and Rosecrans plotted strategy. Both commanders decided on a morning attack against the enemy right flank. Rosecrans scheduled his assault to commence at 7 a.m. after his troops had eaten breakfast, while Bragg told his subordinates to strike at dawn. Thus the Confederates seized the initiative, which they would maintain throughout the battle.

Seven grayclad brigades numbering 11,000 men hit the ill-prepared Union right at first light on December 31. "It seemed that the whole Confederate army burst out of a piece of woods immediately on the front," thought a Northern soldier. Troops from Lt. Gen. William J. Hardee's corps drove a Federal division from the field in virtual rout. The next Union division put up more of a fight, and fresh Confederate soldiers led by Lt. Gen. Leonidas Polk joined Hardee's assault. Eventually the combined Confederate pressure overwhelmed the stubborn defenders, and they too fled northward toward the Nashville Pike, Rosecrans's lifeline to supplies and reinforcements.

In the meantime the Union commander persisted in his plan to attack the Confederate right across Stones River. He sent two divisions toward a position east of the stream occupied by Maj. Gen. John C. Breckinridge's troops. Only when frantic pleas for help arrived from his right flank commander did Rosecrans cancel the offensive and redeploy his strength toward the danger point.

Brig. Gen. Philip Sheridan bought valuable time for Rosecrans by repulsing several

≈≈ BATTLE FACTS ≈≈

Battle dates	December 31, 1862 & January 2, 1863
Combat strength	U.S. 43,400; C.S. 37,700
Casualties	U.S. 13,200; C.S. 10,300
Commanders	U.S. Maj. Gen. William S. Rosecrans C.S. Gen. Braxton Bragg

determined Confederate attacks and conducting a fighting withdrawal toward the Nashville Pike. Despite Bragg's success his divisions suffered horrific casualties and they began to lose momentum. Bragg called on Breckinridge to reinforce Hardee and Polk, but Breckinridge balked. The former U.S. Vice President believed he still faced an immediate threat, when in fact Rosecrans had already withdrawn from his portion of the battlefield. Breckinridge's mistake may have cost the Confederates a victory.

By noon the Federals had stabilized their line in a jackknife configuration with the apex in a four-acre oak grove known as the Round Forest. Col. William B. Hazen held this position for the Federals, an area the soldiers would call Hell's Half Acre. Breckinridge at last shifted four brigades across Stones River, and late in the afternoon General Polk fed them piecemeal to the Yankees in the Round Forest. Breckinridge's assaults, delivered with spirit and valor like all the Southern efforts that day, failed to break the Union line. Darkness ended the combat, which had exacted a tremendous human toll from both armies.

The Confederates had won a tactical victory on December 31, but to Bragg's chagrin, Rosecrans refused to retreat. The armies spent January 1 adjusting their lines and shivering in the cold.

Again on January 2 Bragg expected to find the Federals gone, but Rosecrans stood fast. Concerned about Union infantry and artillery, which had crossed Stones River on his right and threatened a flanking fire against the Confederate army, Bragg told Breckinridge to drive the intruders back across the stream. The unfortunate Breckinridge protested this impossible assignment, but executed Bragg's orders at 4 p.m.

Surprisingly Breckinridge succeeded in pushing the Federals off a gentle ridge toward Stones River. His men erred by pursuing their

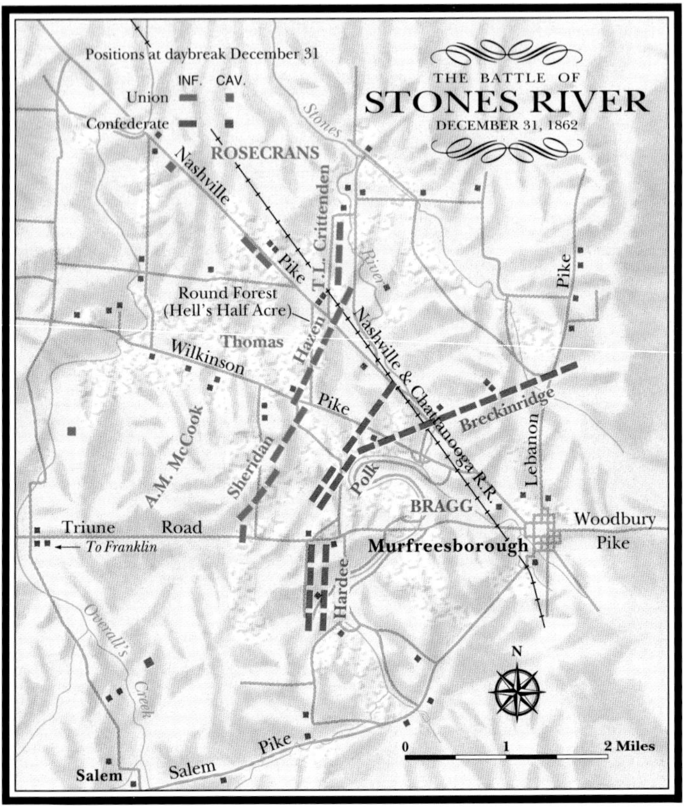
THE BATTLE OF
STONES RIVER
DECEMBER 31, 1862
Positions at daybreak December 31
INF. CAV.
Union
Confederate
ROSECRANS
Nashville Pike
T.L. Crittenden
Stones River
Round Forest
(Hell's Half Acre)
Thomas
Wilkinson Pike
Hazen
Nashville & Chattanooga R.R.
Pike
Breckinridge
Lebanon Pike
A.M. McCook
Sheridan
Polk
BRAGG
Triune Road
To Franklin
Murfreesborough
Woodbury Pike
Hardee
Overall's Creek
N
0 1 2 Miles
Salem
Salem Pike

retreating foes. Maj. John Mendenhall had collected 57 guns across the stream and raked the charging graycoats with devastating effectiveness. The Confederates "opened the door of Hell," observed one witness, "and the devil himself was there to greet them." When Union infantry counterattacked, the Southerners fled back to their starting point, losing 1,700 men in 45 minutes.

Ignoring the advice of his generals, Bragg declined to retreat that night. On January 3, however, he agreed to abandon Murfreesboro and fall back to the south, promptly carrying out a skillful withdrawal. His losses had been grievous: 27 percent of his 37,700 men killed, wounded, or missing.

Rosecrans also lost heavily: a total of 13,200 casualties. But the Union commander held the more valid claim to the victory declared by both armies. The engagement solidified Union control of Kentucky and secured Nashville for the North. Bragg's retreat encouraged Unionists in east Tennessee and depressed Confederate sympathizers in the state. Most of all, the Battle of Stones River provided the Lincoln administration with welcome news amidst the December disasters at Fredericksburg, Virginia, and near Vicksburg, Mississippi. "I can never forget," the President told Rosecrans, "that…you gave us a hard earned victory which, had there been a defeat instead, the nation could scarcely have lived over."

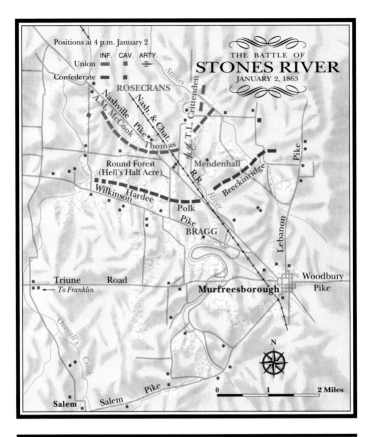

Positions at 4 p.m. January 2

	INF.	CAV.	ARTY.
Union			
Confederate			

THE BATTLE OF
STONES RIVER
JANUARY 2, 1863

ROSECRANS

Nashville Pike

A.M. McCook

Nash. & Chat.

Stones

Thomas

M. T. L. Crittenden

Mendenhall

Breckinridge

Pike

Round Forest
(Hell's Half Acre)

R. R.

River

Wilkinson

Hardee

Polk
Pike
BRAGG

Lebanon

Triune   Road
← To Franklin

Murfreesborough

Woodbury
Pike

Overall's Creek

N

0   1   2 Miles

Salem   Salem   Pike

PARK INFORMATION

HEADQUARTERS: Stones River National Battlefield, 3501 Old Nashville Highway, Murfreesboro, TN 37129. (615) 893-9501.

DIRECTIONS: Located 27 miles southeast of Nashville. From Nashville, take I-24 south to exit 78B, follow Tenn. 96 to US 41/70S (Broad St.), turn left and follow signs. From Chattanooga, take I-24 north to exit 78.

SCHEDULE: Open daily from 8 a.m. to 5 p.m. Closed Christmas.

ENTRANCE FEE: None

TOURS: Visitors may take self-guided auto tour past 9 tour stops. Audiotape to accompany tour is available at Visitor Center. Two-and five-mile hiking trails through battlefield.

POINTS OF INTEREST:
■ **Rosecrans's Headquarters Site** One mile northwest of Visitor Center. ■ **Bragg's Headquarters Site** One mile southeast of Visitor Center. ■ **Redoubt Brannan** Built by Union after battle as supply base. Located southeast of Visitor Center. Soon to be open to public.

NEARBY HISTORIC INNS: Bed and Breakfast Hospitality Tennessee, P. O. Box 110227, Nashville, TN 37222; (615) 331-5244 or (800) 458-2421. Statewide reservation service for historic inns.

CHATTANOOGA

Maj. Gen. William S. Rosecrans and 40,000 weary survivors of the Battle of Chickamauga took refuge in Chattanooga, Tennessee, in late September 1863. Rosecrans's Union army might have continued its retreat northwest to Nashville, a withdrawal which would have entailed risk and isolated a smaller Northern force in Knoxville. Instead, threatened by Gen. Braxton Bragg's victorious army, Rosecrans constructed works that described a narrow arc protecting Chattanooga and awaited help.

Help was indeed on the way in the form of two corps from Virginia under Maj. Gen. Joseph Hooker and four divisions from Vicksburg by way of Memphis led by Maj. Gen. William T. Sherman. However, unless Rosecrans could devise a way to supply his army, reinforcements would be of little use.

After Chickamauga, Bragg did

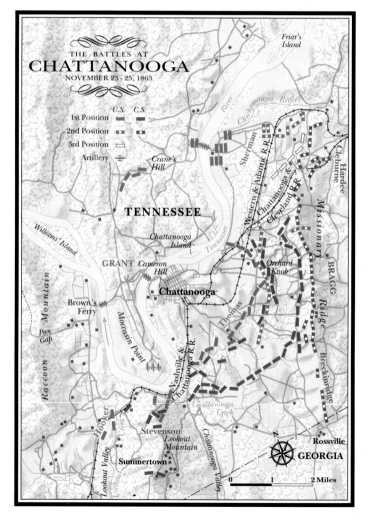

BATTLE FACTS

Battle dates	November 23–25, 1863
Combat strength	U.S. 70,000; C.S. 46,200
Casualties	U.S. 5,800; C.S. 6,700
Commanders	U.S. Maj. Gen. Ulysses S. Grant C.S. Gen. Braxton Bragg

not immediately pursue his beaten enemy. But when the Confederates at last arrived opposite Chattanooga, they placed a stranglehold on the city's rail and river supply lines. Part of Bragg's army occupied 500-foot-high Missionary Ridge, which overlooks Chattanooga from the east and south. The Confederates then stretched across the valley of Chattanooga Creek and up the slopes of Lookout Mountain southwest of town. As a result, Rosecrans's only means of communications wound 60 rugged miles from his railhead at Stevenson, Alabama, up the Sequatchie Valley, over a spur of the Cumberland Mountains, and across the Tennessee River into Chattanooga from the north. Bragg unleashed cavalry raids against this thin lifeline, and Rosecrans's soldiers subsisted on starvation rations.

Into this desperate situation stepped Maj. Gen. Ulysses S. Grant. Grant received command of all Union armies in the West in mid-October and hurried to Chattanooga on the 23rd to take personal charge. Before he arrived, he replaced the unfortunate Rosecrans with the hero of Chickamauga, Maj. Gen. George H. Thomas. Thomas vowed to hold Chatta-

nooga "till we starve," but Grant aimed to ensure that such sacrifices would be unnecessary.

Thomas's chief engineer devised a plan, approved by Grant, to lift the siege by capturing Brown's Ferry, a point on the Tennessee River below Chattanooga. If the Confederates controlling Brown's Ferry were subdued, Union steamboats could transport supplies upriver from Alabama and shorten the overland route to eight miles.

In the predawn hours of October 27, 5,000 bluecoats silently arrived at Brown's Ferry, some in pontoon boats that had glided with the current from Chattanooga. They scattered the astonished Confederates and secured a bridgehead. Part of Hooker's force appeared during the day, turning back a determined attack at Wauhatchie on the night of October 28–29. As supplies began to flow over what the soldiers called the "Cracker Line," Bragg's chance to reduce Chattanooga evaporated.

Bragg faced bigger problems than a lost chance at glory. The high command in the Army of Tennessee all despised him, and Bragg dealt with this crisis by ridding himself of several malcontents. After dismissing two corps commanders and various lesser lights, he welcomed President Davis, his staunch supporter, to the army's camp on October 9. Davis hoped to restore harmony, but his initiative failed. Bragg's generals unanimously told the President that they lacked confidence in their commander. Davis, however, refused to act. He not only sustained his unpopular field commander, he devised an expedient to rid the army of Bragg's most persistent critic.

Lt. Gen. James Longstreet had arrived at Chickamauga with two divisions of the Army of Northern Virginia and a reputation as one of the South's best soldiers. Never one to suppress his opinions, he voiced his disapproval of Bragg's post-Chickamauga generalship. "Lee's old war horse" carried too much prestige to banish, so at Davis's suggestion Bragg ordered Longstreet to conduct an offensive against Knoxville. That city did possess strategic value, and the Union army there might be beaten, but Bragg's principal motivation was to remove the nettlesome Longstreet from his army. On November 5 Longstreet left for Knoxville with 15,000 troops— men badly needed to oppose Grant at Chattanooga.

In mid-November, with the siege lifted and Sherman's veterans at last on the scene, Grant prepared to move. He had 70,000 men available to face only 46,200 remaining graycoats. His target would be the northern end of Missionary Ridge, known as Tunnel Hill, behind which ran Bragg's supply line to the south. Grant assigned his friend Sherman the responsibility for the primary offensive. Hooker would move around or through the Confederate defenses at Lookout Mountain, cross the Chattanooga Valley, and occupy Rossville Gap, threatening Bragg's left on Missionary Ridge. Thomas would remain in reserve in the center, prepared to exploit a breakthrough on either of Bragg's flanks.

On November 23, a part of Thomas's force captured Orchard Knob, a modest plateau midway between Chattanooga and Missionary Ridge. Grant extended his lines outward and waited for Sherman's surprise thrust against Bragg's right. The following day, Sherman pushed 26,000 soldiers toward Tunnel Hill. Much to his chagrin, he discovered that a deep valley separated his troops from their objective. To make matters worse, the veteran division of Maj. Gen. Patrick R. Cleburne, recently recalled by Bragg from an aborted mission to reinforce Longstreet, blocked his path. Sherman deployed in the difficult terrain and prepared to attack in the morning.

Meanwhile Hooker achieved more success at Lookout Mountain. Using 10,000 men from three divisions, Hooker attacked 7,000 scattered Confederate defenders. Heavy fog obscured the view of Lookout Mountain from Chattanooga, prompting one Federal to call the engagement the "battle above the clouds." By nightfall, the Southerners had been bested. Bragg ordered them to join the main Confederate line on Missionary Ridge. The following morning, Hooker raised the American flag at the mountain's summit and moved into the Chattanooga Valley toward Rossville Gap.

Sherman's attacks against Tunnel Hill commenced about 10 a.m.

November 25. "Every discharge plowed huge gaps through the lines…as these brave troops moved forward with a steadiness and order which drew… admiration from those who witnessed it," recalled a Confederate. In spite of this tenacity, Cleburne's superb warriors repulsed each of Sherman's assaults. By midafternoon Sherman counted 2,000 casualties and was no closer to Tunnel Hill than he had been at dawn. Regretfully, he sent word to Grant that he could do no more.

Hooker moved slowly across the Chattanooga Valley, delayed by the need to bridge Chattanooga Creek. At 3:00 p.m. he reached Rossville Gap. As he began operations against Bragg's left, daylight was waning. Grant, impatient with events and concerned about Sherman's security, ordered Thomas to advance four divisions from Orchard Knob toward the center of Missionary Ridge to relieve the pressure on Sherman.

Bragg had prepared three defensive lines on Missionary Ridge. The first protected the base of the heights. Intermediate works, only partially completed, sheltered additional troops, and the third line followed the ridgetop. Unfortunately for Bragg, his engineers positioned the upper line on the topographical rather than the military crest, meaning that pockets of "dead space," out of range of the defenders, existed on the slopes. The Missionary Ridge position, though seemingly invulnerable, possessed fatal flaws.

Thomas's troops marched magnificently toward the Confederate line shouting "Remember Chickamauga!" In a flash, they overran the first row of trenches, achieving their immediate mission.

It became apparent, however, that to remain at the base of the ridge would be suicidal. "A few minutes of such terrific, telling fire would quickly convert [the captured trenches] into untenable hideous slaughter pens," wrote an officer. So the blue wave impulsively surged up the hill, to the shock of both the Confederates above and Grant on Orchard Knob. The panic-stricken Southerners raced for safety, leaving 37 guns and 2,000 prisoners in Union hands. Cleburne's gritty rearguard defense concluded the battles for Chattanooga.

Grant lost more than 5,800 men in the engagements around Chattanooga; Bragg lost 6,700. Union control of the city denied the Confederacy an important link in their east-west communications. It also set the stage for the Atlanta Campaign and provided Grant a boost toward his elevation to general-in-chief in March. Finally, the defeat at Chattanooga at last convinced Jefferson Davis that he could no longer afford the earnest but ineffective Braxton Bragg in field command. Bragg tendered his resignation a few days after the battle and, for better or worse, joined Davis in Richmond as the President's military adviser.

PARK INFORMATION

HEADQUARTERS: Chickamauga and Chattanooga National Military Park, P. O. Box 2128, Fort Oglethorpe, GA 30742. Telephone: (706) 866-9241.

For park information see Chickamauga, page 23.

VIRGINIA

Virginia's human and material resources proved crucial in the Confederacy's four-year defense against superior Northern power. After casting its electoral vote for Unionist John Bell in 1860, the state resisted aligning with more radical Southern states until after President Lincoln's call for troops. The state convention voted 88 to 55 for secession on April 17, 1861, making Virginia the first state in the Upper South to leave the Union. On May 20, the Confederate Congress in Montgomery, Alabama, resolved that the capital should be moved to Richmond. From the summer of 1861 on, Richmond and Virginia often occupied center stage in the national drama.

The colossus of the Confederacy, Virginia ranked first in wealth, population, and military-age white manpower. Its industrial output nearly equaled that of the entire Deep South and a fifth of the Confederacy's railroad mileage ran within its borders. Its mines yielded more coal, iron, salt, and lead than those of any other Southern state. The massive Tredegar Iron Works of Richmond turned out a multitude of armaments and hardware vital to the Confederate war effort. Virginia's

▼ *Hillsman House, Sailor's Creek*

farms were no less important, especially in the grain-rich Shenandoah Valley, which both sides sought to control through much of the war.

Out of an 1860 population of 1,047,411 whites (355,526 living in what became West Virginia), Virginia probably contributed at least 100,000 men to the Confederacy. Although no precise figures survive, the state's Confederate dead likely approached 25,000. Another 31,872 white Virginians, the vast majority hailing from western counties, fought for the North, as did 5,919 of the state's 432,711 enslaved and 58,042 free blacks. No other state matched Virginia's roster of 91 Confederate generals, headed by such luminaries as Robert E. Lee, Thomas J. "Stonewall" Jackson (born in present-day West Virginia), Joseph E. Johnston, and Jubal A. Early. The Union counted Winfield Scott, George H. Thomas, and 16 other Virginians among its generals.

Virginia witnessed military activity on a singularly enormous scale—more than 2,150 engagements. From the first large battle at Manassas on July 21, 1861, through the nine-month siege of Petersburg in 1864–65, the war's most famous armies repeatedly took each other's measure. A succession of Union commanders came to grief against Lee's Army of Northern Virginia at the Seven Days' Battles, Second Manassas, Fredericksburg, and Chancellorsville, while Grant and the Army of the Potomac hammered their way south from the Wilderness to Cold Harbor in May and June of 1864.

Other memorable battles included the Union debacle at Ball's Bluff on October 21, 1861, which sparked political turmoil in Washington; Cedar Creek on October 19, 1864, where Lt. Gen. Jubal A. Early's Confederates routed two-thirds of Maj. Gen. Philip H. Sheridan's larger force before suffering a shattering defeat; and Sailor's Creek on April 6, 1865, where much of Lee's retreating army disintegrated. The end of the war in Virginia came on April 9, 1865, when Lee surrendered the remnant of his army to Grant at Appomattox Court House.

National Historic Landmarks

BALL'S BLUFF
For information, contact:
Northern Virginia Regional
    Park Authority
5400 Ox Road
Fairfax, VA 22039
(703) 352-5900
Located just north of Leesburg, south of the Potomac River.

CEDAR CREEK and
BELLE GROVE
For information, contact:
Cedar Creek Battlefield
    Foundation, Inc.
Box 229
Middletown, VA 22645
(703) 869-2064
Located between Middletown and Strasburg on US 11.

SAILOR'S CREEK
For information, contact:
Twin Lakes State Park
Route 2, Box 70
Green Bay, VA 23942
(804) 392-3435
Located 56 miles west of Petersburg on Va. 617.

MANASSAS

The spring of 1861 saw thousands of 90-day volunteers flock to Washington to suppress the rebellion, a process most thought would be very brief. Brig. Gen. Irvin McDowell organized the largest army ever assembled in North America, 35,000 strong, and reluctantly heeded his superiors' directives to launch an offensive against the Confederate capital. "On to Richmond" clamored the headlines, and on July 16 McDowell led his ill-trained citizen-soldiers into the Virginia countryside.

His immediate goal, Manassas Junction, lay 29 miles to the southwest. The village possessed military significance because railroads leading from Washington, the Virginia Piedmont, and the Shenandoah Valley converged there. A Confederate army of 22,000 under Brig. Gen. P. G. T. Beauregard defended Manassas behind a meandering stream named Bull Run.

Although he was outnumbered, Beauregard could look to the lower Shenandoah Valley for reinforcements. Near Winchester, 50 miles northwest of Manassas, a Confederate army of 12,000 commanded by Brig. Gen. Joseph E. Johnston faced 18,000 Union soldiers under Maj. Gen. Robert Patterson. If Johnston could elude Patterson, his arrival at Manassas would even the odds for the Southerners.

Confederate spies brought Beauregard immediate news of McDowell's departure. The general relayed this information to Richmond, where the War Department ordered Johnston to transfer his army to Manassas. Johnston's stealth and Patterson's lack of vigilance enabled the Confederates to slip away before dawn on July 18. Johnston's First Brigade, Virginians under Brig. Gen. Thomas J. Jackson, arrived at Manassas the next afternoon. They traveled part of the way by train. On July 21 the same line would rush troops to a battlefield they could not have reached by any other means, and they would turn the course of the fight—a first in the history of military tactics.

Meanwhile McDowell reached Bull Run and probed Beauregard's position along the south bank. McDowell's clumsy reconnaissance demonstrated that the Confederate center and right, his intended targets, were too strong to assail. The Union commander pondered his options as, unknown to him, more of Johnston's troops detrained at Manassas.

BATTLE FACTS
First Manassas

Battle date	July 21, 1861
Combat strength	U.S. 28,500; C.S. 32,200
Casualties	U.S. 2,700; C.S. 2,000
Commanders	U.S. Brig. Gen. Irvin McDowell
	C.S. Brig. Gen. Joseph E. Johnston
	Brig. Gen. P. G. T. Beauregard

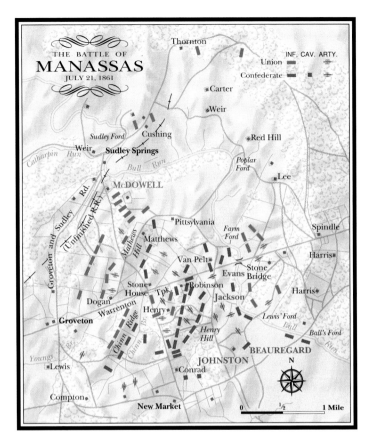

At last McDowell decided to sweep beyond the Confederate left before dawn on July 21, cross Bull Run at an unguarded ford, and move against the enemy's rear. His plan had merit, but poor execution by undisciplined soldiers and inexperienced officers caused delays. The first Union troops did not appear at Sudley Ford until 9 a.m., and by then Confederate signal stations had detected their presence.

Beauregard and Johnston also intended to attack the enemy's left, so they had concentrated most of their strength downstream. Only a small brigade under Col. Nathan G. Evans, guarding the stone bridge on the Warrenton Turnpike, could meet the sudden Union threat. Evans moved northwest to Matthews Hill to contest the approach of 15,000 Federal troops.

Evans fought heroically, assisted by other Confederate units, but by noon fresh Northern troops drove them south across the Warrenton Turnpike to Henry Hill. "Victory! Victory! The day is ours!" shouted an ecstatic McDowell, who halted at the base of Henry Hill to realign his forces.

This pause gave the Confederates a chance to form a new defense, out of sight of the Federals, just over the crest of the plateau. They rallied around Jackson's brigade, which Confederate Brig. Gen. Barnard E. Bee likened to a stone wall. Legend obscures exactly what Bee said, but the name stuck to the brigade and its commander, whose determination helped turn the tide of battle.

About 2 p.m. McDowell resumed his offensive by ordering two artillery batteries supported by infantry onto Henry Hill. Confederate fire dispersed the infantry. Then one of Jackson's regiments approached the guns. Confused by the Virginians' blue uniforms, the Federals held their fire and were swept by a murderous volley. The entire Confederate line advanced, and for two hours the battle swayed back and forth across the hilltop.

Johnston's last arrivals from the Valley struck the exposed Union right flank about 4 p.m. "A panic…seized all the troops within sight," remembered a Union brigade commander. "The men seemed to be seized simultaneously by the conviction that it was no use to do anything more and they might as well start home."

The retreat began with reasonable efficiency, but when a shell demolished a wagon, blocking a bridge on the main withdrawal

route, chaos erupted. Some civilians who had ridden out from Washington to enjoy a Union victory were caught in the dash for safety. Jackson and others urged pursuit but Johnston demurred. The Confederates' disorganization and exhaustion matched the Federals', allowing McDowell to patch together a defensive perimeter near Centreville while his army retreated to Washington.

The First Battle of Manassas (called Bull Run in the North) claimed 5,000 casualties, modest by late-war standards but thoroughly shocking in 1861. The Confederate victory left the South overconfident and the North committed to avenging its disgrace. More importantly it awakened rational thinkers on both sides to the likelihood of a long war.

Perhaps the man to achieve victory in that war, thought President Lincoln, was Maj. Gen. George B. McClellan. McClellan arrived in Washington days after the Manassas debacle. By the spring of 1862, he recruited, trained, and equipped a 100,000-man force he called the Army of the Potomac.

▾ *Chinn Ridge, Second Manassas*

BATTLE FACTS
Second Manassas

Battle dates	August 29–30, 1862
Combat strength	U.S. 63,000; C.S. 55,000
Casualties	U.S. 14,000; C.S. 8,400
Commanders	U.S. Maj. Gen. John Pope C.S. Gen. Robert E. Lee

McClellan ferried his army to the Virginia Peninsula east of Richmond and began a cautious march toward the Confederate capital. Johnston had no choice but to abandon Manassas and confront this threat. He did, however, leave Jackson in the Shenandoah Valley to prevent three Union armies from reinforcing McClellan.

On May 31 Johnston fell with a serious wound and Gen. Robert E. Lee replaced him as commander of the Army of Northern Virginia. In one month Lee, joined by Jackson's triumphant "foot cavalry," drove McClellan from the gates of Richmond to a haven on the James River.

While Lee bested McClellan east of Richmond, Lincoln created the Army of Virginia from the luckless units victimized by Jackson in the Valley. The President chose an aggressive, bombastic Illinois general named John Pope to lead these 47,000 men.

Convinced that McClellan would not renew his advance against Richmond, Lee dispatched Jackson in mid-July to face Pope. A month later McClellan began to withdraw from the Peninsula. Lee now determined that he must defeat Pope before McClellan's army reached northern Virginia, where the two Union forces could combine in overwhelming numbers.

Lee marched northwest to the Rapidan River with his other wing commander, Maj. Gen. James Longstreet, increasing the reunited Confederate army to 55,000 troops. Pope fell back behind the Rappahannock River. Here, reinforced by the vanguard of McClellan's army, he established an impenetrable defense. Prevented from going through Pope, Lee opted to go around him. On August 25 he sent Jackson's wing on a 56-mile flank march that reached Pope's supply base at Manassas before daybreak on August 27. Hungry Confederates enjoyed their richest feast of the war, then torched what they could not carry away.

Pope eagerly ordered his army to converge on Jackson and "bag" the Confederates. Unfortunately for the Federals, they could not find their quarry. Stonewall had hidden behind the bed of an unfinished railroad north of the old Manassas battlefield. On August 28 he emerged to strike isolated Federal units at the Battle of Brawner's Farm, inflicting and sustaining frightful losses.

Pope now assumed he had Jackson cornered and prepared to annihilate the Confederates before they could escape. In his zeal to punish Jackson, Pope completely ignored the rest of the Confederate army. Longstreet and Lee followed Stonewall's route, arriving on Jackson's right before noon on August 29. Unaware of their proximity, Pope confidently assailed Jackson's line behind the unfinished railroad. The Union attacks came in uncoordinated waves, and Jackson repulsed them all.

At dawn on the 30th, certain as ever that Longstreet had not arrived, Pope again believed the Confederates to be in retreat. He organized a "pursuit" that turned into another series of frontal charges against Jackson's old position. Stonewall's men stood firm, throwing rocks when they exhausted their ammunition, but at last called on Longstreet to assist them.

Longstreet responded at 4 p.m. with a powerful assault that swept the Federals east to the high ground at Chinn Ridge. Five Union brigades resisted long enough for other units to rally on Henry Hill, where attempts to dislodge them failed before dark. That night Pope's dispirited

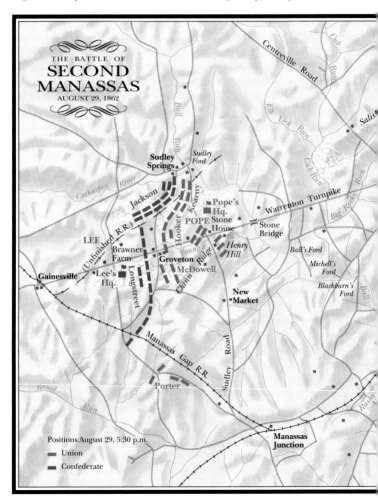

THE BATTLE OF
SECOND MANASSAS
AUGUST 29, 1862

Positions August 29, 5:30 p.m.
- Union
- Confederate

soldiers retraced the bitter retreat of 13 months earlier, this time in relatively good order.

The dimensions of the battle dwarfed First Manassas. Pope lost 14,000 men to Lee's 8,400.

As he had after First Manassas, Lincoln turned to McClellan to rescue Union fortunes. Now, however, the Confederates assumed the initiative. In early September Lee launched his first offensive across the Potomac River. That campaign would end two weeks later along the banks of Maryland's Antietam Creek.

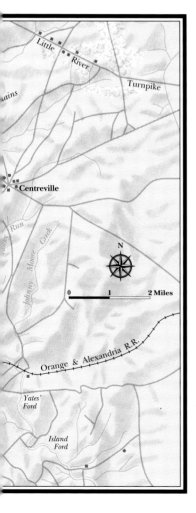

PARK INFORMATION

HEADQUARTERS: Manassas National Battlefield Park, 6511 Sudley Road, Manassas, VA 22110. (703) 361-1339.

DIRECTIONS: From Washington, D.C., take I-66 west to Va. 234 north (Sudley Rd.) at exit 47. Proceed 3/4 of mile to Visitor Center on right.

SCHEDULE: Park grounds open daily during daylight hours. Visitor Center open daily from 8:30 a.m. to 5 p.m. and from mid-June to Labor Day until 6 p.m. Closed Christmas.

ENTRANCE FEE: Ages 17–61, $1.00.

TOURS: One-mile, self-guided walking tour over Henry Hill, critical area of fighting during First Manassas. Interpretive markers, audio stations, and artillery positions along way. Twelve-mile, self-guided auto tour takes visitors through larger Second Manassas battlefield. Park maps and audiocassettes available at Visitor Center. Hiking and bridle trails throughout park. Guided tours offered by park rangers in summer and on weekends rest of year, weather permitting. Schedule group tours in advance.

POINTS OF INTEREST:
■ **Visitor Center** Museum houses exhibits of Manassas battles, slide program, battle map program, and bookstore.
■ **Stone House Tavern** Used as Union field hospital. Marker 2 of Second Manassas tour.

NEARBY HISTORIC INNS: Loudoun County Conf. & Visitor Bureau, 108-D South Street SE, Leesburg, VA 22075; (703) 777-0519. Regional reservation service for historic inns.

SEVEN DAYS

The Seven Days' Battles of June and July 1862 rescued Richmond, Virginia, the Confederate capital, from what looked to be certain capture. In late March the Army of the Potomac, numbering 100,000 men under Union Maj. Gen. George B. McClellan, landed at Fort Monroe on the Virginia Peninsula. Two months later the Federals arrived on Richmond's doorstep, seven miles east of the Confederate White House.

The Northern commander, known in some circles as the "young Napoleon," intended to mount his heavy siege artillery and bombard Richmond into submission. But McClellan's advance bogged down on roads rendered impassable by heavy rains. Moreover, the chronically overcautious general believed that Richmond's defenders outnumbered him two to one. A fierce but unsuccessful Confederate attack at Fair Oaks on May 31 and June 1 further convinced McClellan that he needed help.

The Confederates reaped far greater consequences from Fair Oaks. Gen. Joseph E. Johnston, one of the heroes of First Manassas and leader of the main Rebel army in Virginia, sustained serious wounds at the battle. President Jefferson Davis replaced him with Gen. Robert E. Lee, a presidential military adviser.

Lee inherited about 50,000 men, more a collection of individual divisions than a unified army. He assumed his post with little acclaim and modest expectations from the press and public. Although Lee possessed a sterling reputation in the prewar army, his performance in various Confederate assignments had been undistinguished. His troops called him "Granny Lee" or the "King of Spades" behind his back, referring to his conservative demeanor and

BATTLE FACTS

Battle dates	June 25–July 1, 1862
Combat strength	U.S. 91,200; C.S. 95,500
Casualties	U.S. 16,000; C.S. 21,000
Commanders	U.S. Maj. Gen. George B. McClellan C.S. Gen. Robert E. Lee

▲ *Malvern Hill*

emphasis on building fortifications. McClellan considered Lee "too cautious & weak under grave responsibility [and] likely to be timid & irresolute in action." Seldom was an assessment more inaccurate. Within three weeks McClellan would learn how poorly he had judged his new opponent.

Lee immediately constructed eight miles of earthworks running north from White Oak Swamp to the Chickahominy River and then along the south bank of that marshy, swollen stream. Reaching north toward expected reinforcements, McClellan posted troops on both sides of the Chickahominy, across which a number of makeshift bridges precariously linked his divided army.

Lee knew that if he waited until Little Mac received fresh divisions and deployed his huge guns, Richmond would be doomed. He needed to force the action and thought the Federal wing north of the Chickahominy offered an inviting target. Hoping to pinpoint the

Union dispositions, Lee instructed his cavalry commander, Brig. Gen. James Ewell Brown "Jeb" Stuart, to reconnoiter around McClellan's right. On June 12 Stuart embarked on an adventure that covered a hundred miles in three days and completely encircled the Army of the Potomac. The exhausted cavalier then reported to Lee that the Union flank lay unprotected, prompting the Southern commander to immediately prepare his offensive.

Stonewall Jackson and his 18,500 veterans in the Shenandoah Valley held the key to Lee's strategy. Lee ordered Stonewall to bring his Valley army to Richmond and lead a movement around McClellan's right flank. Jackson's goal was White House Landing on the Pamunkey River, the Union supply base connected to the front by the Richmond & York River Railroad. Lee assigned divisions under Maj. Gens. A. P. Hill,

D. H. Hill, and James Longstreet to assist Jackson, establishing June 26 as the day for the advance.

While 55,000 Confederates executed this envelopment north of the Chickahominy, the remaining Southern troops under Maj. Gen. John B. Magruder would hold the

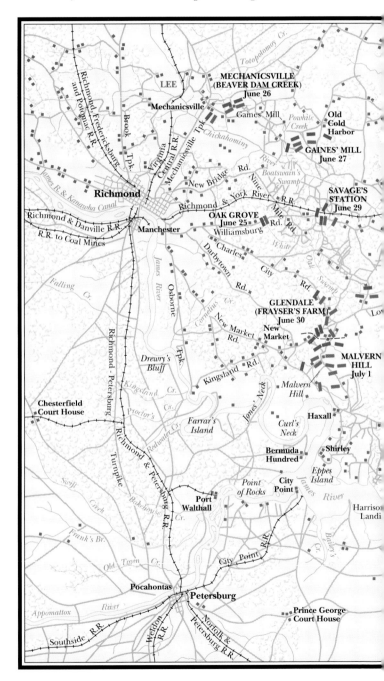

direct line to Richmond south of the river. Lee had accumulated nearly 30,000 men for this task, arguably the more difficult mission.

THE SEVEN DAYS' BATTLES
JUNE 25 - JULY 1, 1862

Pamunkey River

Richmond & York River R.R.

White House

Richmond

idge Rd.

Chickahominy River

CLELLAN

Charles City Court House

James River

Union
Confederate

N

0 1 2 3 4 5 Miles

McClellan counted 60,000 soldiers south of the Chickahominy, more than enough to overpower Magruder and waltz into Richmond. Lee's plan thus entailed great risk.

Ironically, Stuart's glorious ride increased that risk. The Confederate raid highlighted the vulnerability of McClellan's supply line from White House Landing, so the Union commander ordered his provisions shifted to Harrison's Landing on the James River. There Union gunboats could ensure their safety. He transferred another corps south of the Chickahominy, leaving only Brig. Gen. Fitz John Porter's Fifth Corps, reinforced to 30,000 troops, north of the river. Porter would guard the old supply network until it became obsolete and wait to meet whatever new units President Lincoln might send overland from Washington.

On June 25 McClellan directed the bulk of his army to advance about a mile and secure a road leading to New Bridge and Porter's isolated wing. The adjustment touched off a small engagement called the Battle of Oak Grove, the beginning of a solid week of fighting known as the Seven Days' Battles.

McClellan's aggression at Oak Grove underscored Lee's tremendous strategic gamble. Would the Federals launch their own attack south of the Chickahominy before the Southern offensive commenced? On the morning of June 26, an anxious Lee waited on a bluff overlooking the river's south bank and the village of Mechanicsville, straining for evidence of Jackson's approach. Stonewall's presence would signal Longstreet and the two Hills to cross the river and, Lee hoped, compel Porter to abandon his outposts in Mechanicsville and his entrenched position behind Beaver Dam Creek. Then Lee's divisions north of the river would move east to a point parallel with Magruder's lines on the south bank, reconnecting the two wings of the Confederate army via New Bridge.

Morning lapsed into afternoon with no sign of Jackson. Stonewall, it turned out, had started late, only to find his route blocked by Union cavalry who had learned of his intentions from a Confederate deserter. Jackson did reach his geographic objective late that afternoon, but finding no supporting columns and hearing nothing from Lee all day, he went into bivouac.

Meanwhile A. P. Hill had grown impatient over the delay. In defiance of orders, Hill moved five brigades across the Chickahominy, driving Porter's pickets away from Mechanicsville. Assisted by some of D. H. Hill's troops, the fiery Virginian then assaulted Porter's impregnable line behind Beaver Dam Creek. In a matter of moments Confederate casualties lay along the streambed "like flies in a bowl of sugar." One Georgia regiment lost 335 out of 514 men, almost as many killed and wounded as Porter lost in his entire corps. The battle petered out at dark, leaving 1,400 Southerners victims of Yankee lead.

The Battle of Mechanicsville was a Confederate tactical disaster. But when Porter discovered Jackson's column near his right flank poised to reach his rear the next day, the Union general withdrew. He halted four miles east behind a waterway called Boatswain's Swamp, where he established a strong defensive perimeter. Mechanicsville also convinced McClellan to forsake his effort to capture Richmond. He directed all the remaining supplies at White House Landing to be transported overland to his new base on the James, shipped out by water, or destroyed. Porter remained north of the Chickahominy on June 27 to protect this operation.

Lee's plans for June 27 mirrored those of the previous day. Once again Jackson would advance beyond the anticipated Federal flank and threaten the supply line to White House Landing. When Porter moved to guard his communications, Longstreet and A. P. Hill would strike him a killing blow.

Unfortunately, Porter had not remained where Lee expected him and had no reason to preserve a supply line that no longer existed. Jackson again appeared late, no calamity because his designated position no longer possessed tactical relevance. The fighting on June 27 diminished into a repetition of the debacle at Beaver Dam Creek. A. P. Hill launched his brave brigades against Porter's fortified hillside with fatal results. Longstreet enjoyed no better success.

Late in the afternoon Jackson cantered into the crossroads known as New Cold Harbor and spotted his commander. "Ah, General. I am very glad to see you," said Lee. "I had hoped to be with you before." Jackson flinched at this mild rebuke. Recognizing that the Confederate attacks had failed to drive Porter across his front, Jackson had already ordered his divisions to "sweep the field with the bayonet." The generals could hear the crescendo of battle from Boatswain's Swamp. "That fire is heavy," Lee observed. "Do you think your men can stand it?"

"They can stand almost anything," replied Stonewall. "They can stand that!"

The Confederates at last coordinated all 56,000 available men for an assault. Never before had a Southern army concentrated as many troops on a single battlefront. As the sun faded behind their backs, several Confederate units achieved simultaneous breakthroughs, although many accounts credit a Texas regiment led by Brig. Gen. John B. Hood with the first penetration. Porter's weary defenders collapsed, fleeing across the Chickahominy under cover of darkness.

The Battle of Gaines' Mill cost Lee 8,800 and Porter 6,800 men—the bloodiest chapter of the Seven Days. It also achieved Lee's first objective. McClellan told his corps commanders that night to abandon their forward positions south of the Chickahominy and withdraw to a fortified camp on the James 26 miles from Richmond. The military situation now became a race. McClellan sought the safety of the navy's guns at Harrison's Landing, while Lee tried to prevent his escape.

The Union retreat route contained two obstacles. White Oak Swamp meandered across the countryside, fordable at several places but promising logistical problems for McClellan's legion of supply vehicles. Once across the swamp, all roads led to a junction called Glendale. Inevitably the Federals would create a bottleneck here as they funneled onto the single road that led south across Malvern Hill to the James.

On June 28 McClellan commenced his "change of base" in masterful fashion, proving that he possessed better skills as an organizer than as a combat officer. Lee spent the day pondering his opponent's destination. After all, the Federals might opt to move east down the Peninsula the same way they had advanced. Thus McClellan enjoyed a 24-hour head start before Lee concluded that the bluecoats were en route to the James River.

Lee designed a convergence of three separate columns at Glendale. A. P. Hill and Longstreet would cross the Chickahominy and make a wide sweep to the southeast, approaching the intersection via the Darbytown and Long Bridge Roads. They could not possibly reach Glendale until June 30, so Maj. Gen. Benjamin Huger on the Charles City Road and Magruder on the Williamsburg Road would pin down the Federal flank and rear respectively to buy time for Longstreet and Hill.

Jackson received orders to cross the Chickahominy and assist Magruder, but early on the afternoon of June 29 a courier arrived instructing Jackson to watch instead for a possible Federal crossing of the lower Chickahominy. Stonewall remained on the north bank while Magruder initiated a bungled battle at a depot called Savage's Station. The Federals easily repulsed the harried Magruder, then continued their retreat after dark. By ten o'clock the next morning all of McClellan's wagons and troops had negotiated White Oak Swamp.

June 30 marked one of Lee's most disappointing days as commander of the Army of Northern Virginia. His planned concentration at Glendale failed; once again the Confederates found themselves attacking a prepared Union position with a fraction of their available troops.

Jackson crossed the Chickahominy and reached White Oak Swamp late in the morning. The Federals had destroyed the bridge, posting 20,000 soldiers on the high ground south of the stream. Exhausted by a lack of sleep, Stonewall showed none of his usual military acumen. He made little attempt to force a passage at the ruined bridge or try alternative crossing points. "Let us at once to bed," he told his staff, "and see if tomorrow we cannot do something."

Huger's column on the Charles City Road encountered a network of fallen trees cut by the retiring Unionists. Rather than clear the tangle, Huger authorized his lead brigade to build a new road around the obstructions. This ridiculous expedient effectively eliminated 9,000 Confederate troops from the Glendale formula.

Now only Hill and Longstreet would face the five Federal divisions arrayed along the crossroads. Fighting began at 5 p.m. and soon grew vicious. "It was muzzle to muzzle, and the powder actually burned the faces of opposing men," wrote a Union colonel. A Virginia regiment captured a Federal general and a Northern artillery battery lost its guns, but in the end the blue line held. Lee witnessed the profitless loss of another 3,300 of his men. During the night the Union army disappeared again.

Their destination lay three miles south at Malvern Hill. This large plateau, about a mile and a half long and three-quarters of a mile wide, rose a hundred feet at its crest. Swamps, ravines, and creeks protected each side of the hill. A Confederate staff officer knew the area and told D. H. Hill of its natural strength. At a conference on the morning of July 1, Hill advised Lee that "If General McClellan is there in force, we had better let him alone." Longstreet scoffed at Hill's trepidation: "Don't get scared, now that we have got him whipped."

Lee agreed with Longstreet. Motivated perhaps by his frustrations the previous day, Lee ordered the army to approach the base of Malvern Hill. There his old nemesis from north of the Chickahominy, Fitz John Porter, had assumed a powerful defensive posture buttressed by 250 artillery pieces.

Longstreet suggested that the Confederates mount their own guns at two advantageous locations and blast the Northern cannoneers off the hill. Lee authorized the artillery bombardment, instructing his infantry to follow the barrage with an attack. Brig. Gen. Lewis Armistead's brigade received the unenviable responsibility for determining the success of the cannonade and leading the assault "with a yell," the signal for the rest of the army to charge.

The Confederate plan failed miserably. Porter's guns pulverized Longstreet's attempt to unlimber his batteries and the expected Confederate fire never materialized. More serious problems arose at 4 p.m. when officers on each Confederate flank mistakenly reported that Armistead had made his advance, weakening the Federals. Nothing of the sort had occurred, but Lee seized the apparent opportunity and told his subordinates to "press forward your whole line and follow up Armistead's successes."

"I doubt whether, in the annals of war," wrote George McClellan, "there was ever a more persistent and gallant attack, or a more cool and effective resistance." In a familiar pattern intrepid Confederate brigades charged piecemeal into the teeth of superb Union artillery. Some individual graycoats reached Porter's line, but at no time did they threaten to overwhelm it. More often Federal canister raked the Confederate formations as they traversed the gentle slopes, leaving ghastly lines of dead and wounded in neat ranks. "It was not war—it was murder," wrote D. H. Hill, whose own division experienced horrifying casualties. When nightfall ended the slaughter, 5,400 Southerners carpeted the ground, the wounded giving the field "a singular crawling effect."

Despite the victory, and against the wishes of some of his generals, McClellan evacuated Malvern Hill that night and gathered his army at Harrison's Landing. The Seven Days' Battles, all Union tactical triumphs except Gaines' Mill, had cost him 16,000 killed, wounded, or captured. Lee's losses totaled 21,000—nearly one-fourth of his entire force. The general reflected his feelings about the campaign when he wrote, "Under ordinary circumstances, the Federal army should have been destroyed."

Nevertheless, the Seven Days' Battles turned back the most serious "on to Richmond" drive yet mounted. Moreover, Lee used his bloody strategic achievement to seize the initiative in Virginia and move the war from the outskirts of the Confederate capital to north of the Potomac River.

PARK INFORMATION

HEADQUARTERS: Richmond National Battlefield Park, Maggie L. Walker National Historic Site, 3215 East Broad St., Richmond, VA 23223. (804) 226-1981.

DIRECTIONS: Chimborazo Visitor Center (main center) is at 3215 E. Broad St. in Richmond. From Washington, D.C., take I-95S to Exit 74B (US 60, Broad Street), and from Petersburg, head north on I-95 to Exit 74C.

SCHEDULE: Battlefield sites open daily during daylight hours. Chimborazo Visitor Center open daily from 9 a.m. to 5 p.m. Closed Thanksgiving, Christmas, and New Year's Day.

ENTRANCE FEE: None

TOURS: Begin tour at Chimborazo Visitor Center. Audiotapes to rent or purchase accompany 65-mile, self-guided auto tour that follows battles chronologically.

POINTS OF INTEREST:
■ **Chimborazo Visitor Center** Features exhibit rooms, documentary slide show, 30-minute film, and bookshop.
■ **Fort Harrison Visitor Center** Houses small museum.
■ **Cold Harbor Exhibit Shelter** Offers exhibits and electric map program.
■ **Drewry's Bluff** Located on James River. Follow walking trail around site. ■ **Watt House** Landmark during Battle of Gaines' Mill. Restored but not open to public.

NEARBY HISTORIC INNS: Bensonhouse Bed and Breakfast Reservation Service of Virginia, 2036 Monument Ave., Richmond, VA 23220; (804) 353-6900. Statewide reservation service for historic inns.

FREDERICKSBURG *and Spotsylvania*

The peaceful city of Fredericksburg, Virginia, and its surrounding countryside witnessed unprecedented mayhem during the Civil War. Four major battles between 1862 and 1864 left 100,000 casualties strewn across the landscape. The South won signal victories at the first two engagements, Fredericksburg and Chancellorsville. The final two, the Wilderness and Spotsylvania Court House, marked the beginning of an operation that concluded 11 months later in Confederate surrender at Appomattox Court House.

Fredericksburg owed its unenviable distinction as the cockpit of the Civil War to geography. Its 5,000 inhabitants lived precisely midway between Washington and Richmond, the contending capitals. Wagon roads converged at Fredericksburg from all points of the compass, and a railroad connecting the Potomac River with Richmond passed through the colonial city. The Rappahannock River, tidal at Fredericksburg, provided Confederate defenders with a natural moat. West of the town, a 70-square-mile region of scrub oak and pine, known locally as the Wilderness of Spotsylvania, could grip an invading army in a jungly stranglehold. As long as the capture of Richmond dominated Union military thinking in the east,

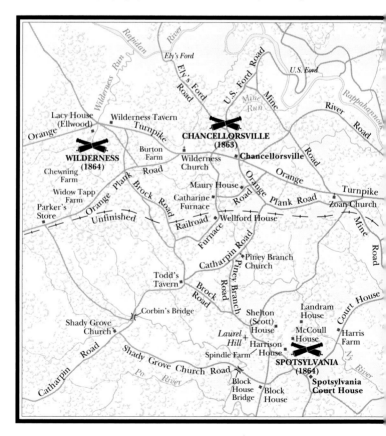

Fredericksburg seemed destined for tragedy.

On November 7, 1862, Maj. Gen. Ambrose E. Burnside inherited command of the Federal Army of the Potomac. Burnside rapidly moved his 115,000 men 40 miles from Warrenton, Virginia, to Stafford Heights, across the Rappahannock River from Fredericksburg. Because the civilian bridges had been destroyed, he needed portable bridges to span the river. A week slipped by before the equipment arrived, and the Unionists missed their chance to cross the river unopposed. In the interim Robert E. Lee and the 78,000 soldiers of the Army of Northern Virginia filed onto the hills behind Fredericksburg and established an imposing defensive position.

Burnside agonized over his options. Both impending winter and political pressure dictated that he act promptly. On December 10 the general (whose whiskers inspired the term sideburns) informed his lieutenants that the army would build six bridges across the Rappahannock: three opposite the city and another three a mile downstream. "There were not two opinions among the subordinate officers as to the rashness of the undertaking," wrote one corps commander, but Burnside ordered the work to commence the following morning.

Under cover of darkness and fog, skilled engineers pushed their pontoons halfway across the icy

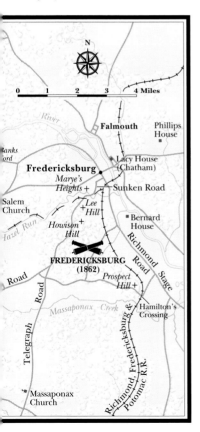

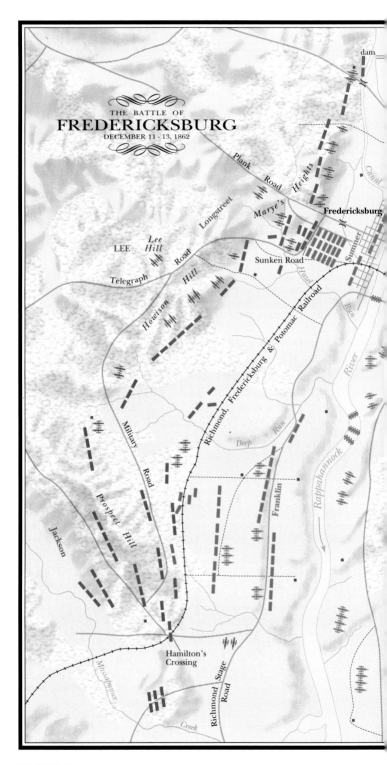

THE BATTLE OF
FREDERICKSBURG
DECEMBER 11 - 13, 1862

dam

Plank Road

Heights

Marye's

Fredericksburg

Canal

LEE

Lee Hill

Longstreet Road

Sumner

Sunken Road

Telegraph

Howison Hill

Richmond, Fredericksburg & Potomac Railroad

Hazel Run

River

Military Road

Deep Run

Prospect Hill

Franklin

Rappahannock River

Jackson

Hamilton's Crossing

Richmond Stage Road

Massaponax

Creek

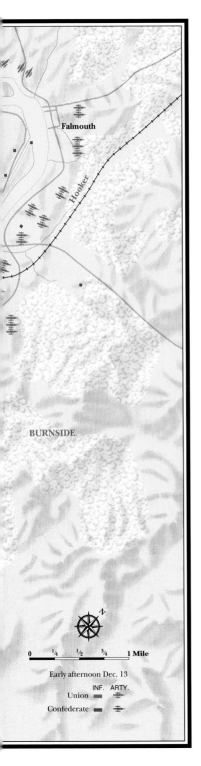

Falmouth

Hooker

BURNSIDE

0   ¼   ½   ¾   1 Mile

Early afternoon Dec. 13

INF. ARTY.

Union

Confederate

Rappahannock. Then the front street of the town erupted in flame as a brigade of Mississippi and Florida troops opened on the bridge builders. After repeated efforts to complete the spans failed, Burnside directed his artillery commander to blast the Confederates out of their lairs. Approximately 150 cannon hurled 8,000 projectiles into the city, but when the smoke cleared the Confederate infantry resumed firing.

Now Burnside called for volunteers to ferry across the Rappahannock, establish a bridgehead, and drive the stubborn Southern riflemen out of the town. Soldiers from Michigan, Massachusetts, and New York accepted the challenge and rowed across the stream. Following a nasty clash in the streets of Fredericksburg, the Yankees secured the city after dark.

Burnside wasted December 12 marching additional divisions into town while some occupiers shamefully looted houses and stores. Lee used the time to summon Stonewall Jackson's corps from its watchful position downstream. The rest of the Confederate army under James Longstreet shifted northward, making room for Jackson and perfecting a seven-mile front bristling with artillery.

The Federal commander authorized an attack the next morning. He called for his Left Grand Division under Maj. Gen. William B. Franklin to move against Jackson south of Fredericksburg, seize the high ground at Prospect Hill, and wheel right, rolling up the Confederate line. Once Franklin had achieved his mission, the Federal brigades in Fredericksburg would launch their own supporting assaults and drive the remaining defenders in disarray toward Richmond.

■ *The Wilderness*

Burnside's conception, while far from brilliant, had merit. But the cautious Franklin compromised its potential by committing only one division to his attack. Nevertheless, these 4,500 Pennsylvanians discovered a gap in Jackson's line and penetrated the Confederate defense, becoming the only Union troops to experience any measure of success during the battle. Stone-wall responded with a counterattack, and the unsupported Northerners withdrew to their starting point.

The Federals in Fredericksburg suffered a more dismal defeat. Burnside lost confidence in his strategy by noon and directed his Right Grand Division to attack regardless of the outcome on Franklin's front. Wave after wave left the protection of the city, descended a naked slope, and crossed

a canal under punishing artillery fire. They then traversed 400 yards of open ground, aiming toward a ridge called Marye's Heights. Lee had crowned this elevation and the surrounding hills with cannon and lined a sunken road at its base with eager soldiers from Georgia and North Carolina.

"We came forward as though breasting a storm of rain and sleet, our faces and bodies being only half-turned to the storm, our shoulders shrugged," remembered one participant. Fifteen brigades challenged the Confederates concealed behind a stone wall below Marye's Heights. "A chicken could not live on that field when we open on it," boasted one Southerner with almost literal accuracy. When nightfall ended the slaughter, more than 8,000 Union soldiers lay on the frozen ground. No attacker had reached the stone wall.

BATTLE FACTS
Chancellorsville

Battle dates	April 27–May 5, 1863
Combat strength	U.S. 134,000; C.S. 61,000
Casualties	U.S. 17,300; C.S. 12,800
Commanders	U.S. Maj. Gen. Joseph Hooker
	C.S. Gen. Robert E. Lee

The Battle of Fredericksburg would be Lee's most lopsided tactical victory. But in a larger sense it accomplished little for the Confederates. The Union army had been bruised, but not destroyed, and Lee found it difficult to replace his 5,300 casualties or feed his survivors. He knew that the dry roads of spring would bring another "on to Richmond" drive to test his ragged warriors.

Maj. Gen. Joseph Hooker would lead that offensive. Hooker replaced Burnside in January and by April had molded the dispirited Fredericksburg veterans into "the finest army on the planet." His campaign strategy matched his organizational acumen. He ordered one wing of the army to tramp 40 miles upstream on the Rappahannock, cross that river and its major tributary, the Rapidan, at fords west of the Confederate defenses, then sweep east against Lee's left flank. The remainder of Fighting Joe's infantry would bridge the Rappahannock below Fredericksburg and menace the Confederate front as the second blade of a great pincers. "My plans are perfect," declared Hooker, "and when I start to carry them out, may God have mercy on General Lee, for I will have none."

Lee spent the winter in his Fredericksburg trenches but detached part of Longstreet's corps in February to gather food in southern Virginia. When Hooker launched his offensive on April 27, 1863, "Marse Robert" counted only 61,000 men in his ranks, less than half the Federal strength.

On April 30 Hooker with 50,000 soldiers reached a crossroads in the Wilderness ten miles west of Fredericksburg dominated by a brick mansion named Chancellorsville. Lee and Jackson correctly perceived these troops, not the Federals opposite them below the city, to be the main threat. Leaving a reinforced division to hold the Fredericksburg entrenchments, Lee and Jackson rode west with the bulk of their army.

The next morning Jackson met Hooker's cautious but numerically superior forces a few miles east of Chancellorsville. Although the Federals could have overwhelmed Stonewall's advance and did briefly place a column behind the Confederate right near the Rappahannock, Hooker retreated to a defensive perimeter in the tangled woods around Chancellorsville. "I retired from [Hooker's] presence," wrote his second in command, "with the

▶ *Salem Church, Chancellorsville*

belief that my commanding general was a whipped man." Hooker's overconfidence had indeed faded, but whether he was "whipped" depended now on Lee and Jackson.

That night the two Confederate generals met at an obscure cross-roads one mile south of Chancellorsville. Here they devised one of the biggest gambles in American military history. Jackson's corps, about 30,000 men, would follow 12 miles of hidden country roads and secretly deploy opposite the vulnerable Union right flank. Lee would direct the remaining 14,000 troops in a grand bluff designed to divert Hooker's attention while Jackson completed his dangerous trek. Both wings of the divided Confederate army, as well as the detachment back at Fredericksburg, faced possible annihilation if the enemy divined the true situation.

The Federals spotted Jackson's column less than an hour after its departure on May 2 and deduced its destination. But by noon Hooker decided that the Confederates were actually escaping. He relaxed his vigilance on the right and embarked upon pursuit of his "fleeing" opponents, capturing a regiment of Jackson's rearguard near Catharine Furnace. Meanwhile Stonewall arranged his road-weary divisions in three lines opposite the unsuspecting Union Eleventh Corps three miles west of Chancellorsville.

The attack that followed drove the overmatched Yankees more than two miles east. But Union resistance proved sufficiently tenacious to disorganize the victorious Confederates and force Jackson to call a halt to realign his men. Seeking to renew the attack after

dark, Stonewall reconnoitered in front of his corps to ascertain the Federals' whereabouts. When nervous North Carolinians heard Jackson's entourage return, they mistook the group for Union cavalry. A volley rang out in the woods, striking the general in three places. Stretcher-bearers carried him toward a field hospital where surgeons amputated his left arm early the next morning. "Could I have directed events," Lee wrote Jackson, "I should have chosen for the good of the country to be disabled in your stead."

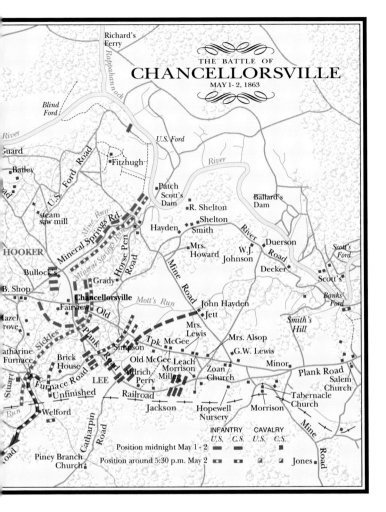

THE BATTLE OF

CHANCELLORSVILLE

MAY 1- 2, 1863

Richard's Ferry

Blind Ford

U.S. Ford

River

Guard

Bailey

Fitzhugh

Patch

Scott's Dam

R. Shelton

Ballard's Dam

steam saw mill

Hayden

Shelton

Smith

Duerson

Scott's Ford

HOOKER

Mrs. Howard

W.J. Johnson

Decker

Bullock's

Grady

B. Shop

Chancellorsville

Mott's Run

John Hayden

Banks' Ford

Fairview

Jett

Smith's Hill

Hazel Grove

Mrs. Lewis

Mrs. Alsop

Sickles

McGee

G.W. Lewis

Minor

Catharine Furnace

Brick House

Simpson

Old McGee

Leach

Zoan Church

Plank Road

Salem Church

Aldrich

Morrison Mills

Stuart

LEE

Perry

Railroad

Tabernacle Church

Unfinished

Jackson

Hopewell Nursery

Morrison

Run

Welford

	INFANTRY		CAVALRY	
	U.S.	C.S.	U.S.	C.S.
Position midnight May 1 - 2				
Position around 5:30 p.m. May 2				

Piney Branch Church

Jones

Despite the reverses of the previous day, Hooker still held the advantage on May 3. As long as he controlled an open plateau called Hazel Grove, he would keep the two wings of Lee's outnumbered army separated and subject to destruction. Jackson's temporary successor, Maj. Gen. J. E. B. Stuart, recognized the peril and prepared to launch a no-holds-barred attack against Hazel Grove at first light.

Hooker made it easy for him. He ordered Hazel Grove abandoned at dawn and withdrew his men to neater lines around a

homestead called Fairview. The most intense fighting of the battle swirled between Hazel Grove and Fairview as brigade after brigade challenged the new Union position. By 10 a.m. the Federal gunners had run low on ammunition. Hooker, stunned by a Confederate cannonball that shattered a portion of his Chancellorsville headquarters, took no steps to replenish the supply. Stuart's troops rushed on to Fairview and then, reunited with Lee, surged into the Chancellorsville clearing. "It must have been from such a scene that men

BATTLE FACTS
The Wilderness

Battle dates	May 5–6, 1864
Combat strength	U.S. 118,000; C.S. 61,000
Casualties	U.S. 18,000; C.S. 7,800
Commanders	U.S. Lt. Gen. Ulysses S. Grant
	Maj. Gen. George G. Meade
	(Army of the Potomac)
	C.S. Gen. Robert E. Lee

in ancient times rose to the dignity of gods," thought a staff officer as powder-stained Confederates wildly cheered their commander.

Lee had little time to enjoy his accolades. A courier now reported that Union troops had overrun the Fredericksburg defenses and were marching west. Lee postponed his plans to dispatch Hooker and sent two divisions east to meet the new crisis. At the Battle of Salem Church on May 3–4, the Confederates drove the advancing Union column back across the Rappahannock. Lee then countermarched to Chancellorsville where he again prepared to assault the main Union army.

But Hooker had given up. Against the wishes of most of his corps commanders, he retreated the next night, arriving on the north bank of the Rappahannock on May 6. The Chancellorsville Campaign cost him 17,300 casualties, considerably more than he had inflicted. Lee's losses, however, crippled a higher percentage of his army and included the indispensable Stonewall Jackson, who died of pneumonia on May 10 at a plantation south of Fredericksburg.

Lee's victory also cleared the way for his cherished desire to take the war north. Two months

after Chancellorsville the Army of Northern Virginia attacked the Federals, now under Maj. Gen. George G. Meade, at Gettysburg in southern Pennsylvania. Lee's devastating defeat forced him to retreat to Virginia. He spent the winter of 1863–64 in Orange County, 35 miles west of Fredericksburg.

The Army of the Potomac wintered across the Rapidan in Culpeper County. In March a new general-in-chief joined them: Lt. Gen. Ulysses S. Grant, summoned by President Lincoln from the western theater. Grant opted to make his headquarters in the field and provided strategic oversight to Meade's army.

The new Union commander subtly altered his predecessors' strategy. Rather than focusing on the capture of Richmond, Grant told Meade to make Lee's army his goal. This objective portended the continuous fighting that would finally bring the Civil War to an end.

On May 4, 1864, Grant sent his soldiers over the Rapidan and into the Wilderness where Hooker had come to grief exactly one year before. He preferred not to fight in the tangled terrain where his two-to-one numerical advantage would be neutralized and planned to steal through the woods before Lee could stop him. The Confederates, however, reacted quickly to Grant's offensive, moving east on two parallel roads to block the Federals.

The Battle of the Wilderness began on May 5 when the Union Fifth Corps discovered Lt. Gen. Richard S. Ewell's Rebel troops dug in on a ridge astride the Orange Turnpike. The battle seesawed back and forth for two days with neither side gaining an advantage.

Four miles south on the Orange Plank Road, another Confederate column brushed aside Federal cavalry on the morning of May 5 and pressed toward the Brock Road, the only north-south thoroughfare in the Wilderness and the link between Grant's scattered corps. Union reinforcements arrived just in time to secure the intersection, then pushed the Confederates back until darkness ended the fighting.

Lee expected the missing third of his army, Longstreet's corps, to appear that night. But by dawn on May 6 "Lee's old war horse" had not arrived, and a powerful Union attack overwhelmed the outgunned Confederate brigades along the Plank Road. Now only a thin line of gray artillery at the Widow Tapp Field stood between the Army of the Potomac and victory.

As the blueclad soldiers approached the clearing, Lee noticed a dusty column swinging east on the Plank Road. "What troops are these?" inquired the anxious commander. "The Texas Brigade!" came the reply. Not a moment too soon, the vanguard of Longstreet's corps had arrived. Lee maneuvered his horse ahead of the deploying Texans (and one Arkansas regiment) as if he intended to lead the attack personally. "Lee to the rear" shouted the soldiers. "We won't go on unless you go back!" For a moment Lee's instincts as a warrior clashed with his duty as commander. Reluctantly he allowed his mount to be guided behind the line of forming infantry. The charge that followed cost the Texans and several other brigades nearly half their men, but arrested the Union momentum.

Now Longstreet seized the initiative. Utilizing the bed of an unfinished railroad south of the Plank Road, he assembled four brigades and marched them opposite the exposed Union left. His sudden attack rolled up the Federals "like a wet blanket." Then

BATTLE FACTS
Spotsylvania

Battle dates	May 7–20, 1864
Combat strength	U.S. 111,000; C.S. 63,000
Casualties	U.S. 18,000; C.S. 10,000
Commanders	U.S. Lt. Gen. Ulysses S. Grant Maj. Gen. George G. Meade (Army of the Potomac) C.S. Gen. Robert E. Lee

a disaster eerily reminiscent of what had happened at Chancellorsville ended Longstreet's offensive. Virginia troops south of the Plank Road accidentally fired on their comrades who had strayed ahead in the thick woods. A party of Confederate officers, including Longstreet, tumbled from their saddles. One Confederate general was killed and Longstreet sustained a debilitating wound. By the time Lee reorganized the attack hours later, Maj. Gen. Winfield S. Hancock had crafted a formidable defense along the Brock Road. Lee's assaults failed.

The dramatic if confusing fighting in the Wilderness claimed 18,000 Federal soldiers. Lee's casualties numbered about half that many. Veterans of the Army of the Potomac had seen this before: a promising new general crosses the rivers, meets Lee, is thrashed, and retreats. But Grant was no Burnside or Hooker. After catching his breath on May 7, he ordered Meade to move southeast after dark toward Spotsylvania Court House. The little county seat occupied a crossroads that controlled the shortest route to Richmond. If Grant could get there first, he would force Lee either to retreat or challenge the Federals on open ground.

Lee wisely anticipated Grant's move toward Spotsylvania and sent Longstreet's corps, now under Maj. Gen. Richard H. Anderson, on a night march to Spotsylvania. Anderson's troops dashed into line two miles from the village on the morning of May 8 seconds before the leading Federal troops struck. The Federals maintained their assaults throughout the day, while reinforcements from both armies

Situation at midnight, May 6 - 7

⬛ Union
⬛ Confederate

erected parallel lines of earthworks.

During the night, Ewell's engineers laid out their entrenchments, which took advantage of the elevated terrain at the edge of a forest. Daybreak revealed that they had created a huge salient, or bulge, protruding north toward the Federals. Because salients could be attacked not only in front but from both sides, officers usually avoided them. Lee, however, opted to retain the position, counting on his artillery to keep the salient safe.

This line, called the Mule Shoe by the soldiers because of its

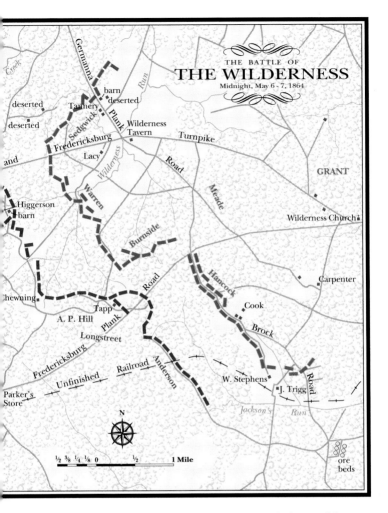

THE BATTLE OF
THE WILDERNESS
Midnight, May 6 - 7, 1864

GRANT

Germanna

Plank

barn
deserted

deserted
Tannery

deserted

Wilderness
Tavern

Turnpike

Sedgwick

Fredericksburg

Lacy

Wilderness

Road

Meade

Wilderness Church

and

Warren

Higgerson
barn

Burnside

Carpenter

Road

Hancock

Chewning

Tapp

A. P. Hill

Cook

Plank

Brock

Longstreet

Fredericksburg

Anderson

Unfinished   Railroad

W. Stephens

J. Trigg

Road

Parker's
Store

Jackson's   Run

N

½ ⅜ ¼ ⅛ 0   ½   1 Mile

ore
beds

shape, dictated the course of the combat at Spotsylvania. Twelve handpicked regiments commanded by a young New Yorker named Emory Upton temporarily pierced the Mule Shoe on May 10. This gave Grant an idea. If 5,000 men could penetrate the salient, what might his entire army accomplish?

The answer came during a 20-hour nightmare remembered as the fight at the Bloody Angle. Grant shifted his army into position on the night of May 11–12, and at first light Hancock's corps

wrested control of most of the Mule Shoe, thanks in part to Lee's ill-advised removal of the Southern artillery the previous night. Beginning at 5:30 a.m. Lee committed every available man to regaining the salient. By 10 a.m. he had restored all but a few hundred yards of his original line.

The Federals spent the rest of the day and most of the night trying to recoup their gains. The fighting concentrated on a tiny patch of ground defended by 1,600 Mississippians and South Carolinians. A shallow valley sliced close to the Confederate line here, providing crucial shelter for swarms of Union assailants. An appalling tactical pattern developed. Successive Federal units would leave their trenches, cross an open field, and take refuge in the swale. From there they kept up a constant rifle fire punctuated by periodic lunges into the works.

The Confederates' elaborate fortifications contributed to miraculous endurance—that and the heroic desperation of half-crazed men whose world consisted of a rain-soaked log pen slippery with the mangled remains of comrades and enemies. "The [Mule Shoe] was a boiling, bubbling and hissing cauldron of death," wrote a Union officer. "Clubbed muskets, and

bayonets were the modes of fighting for those who had used up their cartridges, and frenzy seemed to possess the yelling, demonic hordes on either side."

The bloodbath at the angle bought time for Lee to construct a new line at the base of the salient. At 2 a.m. on May 13, whispered orders reached the front directing the benumbed Confederates to slip silently away from their trenches. Grant's troops took possession of the Bloody Angle at dawn, but Lee's new line rendered it strategically meaningless.

Grant now shifted his army to the left amidst days of heavy downpours, searching for a weak link in the Confederate chain. On May 18 he sent Hancock back to

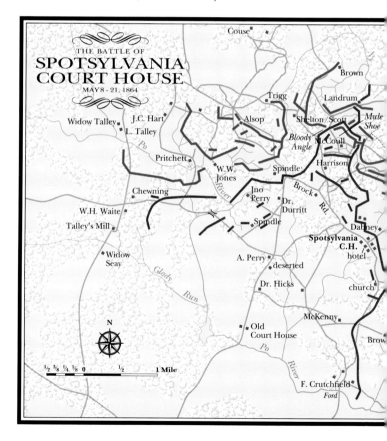

THE BATTLE OF

SPOTSYLVANIA COURT HOUSE

MAY 8 - 21, 1864

the Mule Shoe to catch the enemy by surprise, but the Southerners were ready. Hancock's assault foundered and by midmorning Grant canceled the effort.

Ewell's clumsy reconnaissance on May 19 ended in a sharp action at the Harris Farm, closing the serious fighting at Spotsylvania. The butcher's bill again staggered credulity. Grant suffered 18,000 killed and wounded while Lee lost perhaps 10,000 irreplaceable men. The Federals, bloodied but un-daunted, pushed south again. Lee had no choice but to follow, keep-ing his army between Grant and Richmond. The guns at last fell silent around Fredericksburg. In less than a year, they would be silent everywhere.

PARK INFORMATION

HEADQUARTERS: Fredericksburg and Spotsylvania National Military Park, 120 Chatham Lane, Fredericksburg, VA 22405. (703) 373-4461.

DIRECTIONS: Located on I-95, 50 miles south of Washington, D.C., and 55 miles north of Richmond. From interstate, take exit 45A, Va. 3 east and follow brown signs to Fredericksburg Battlefield Visitor Center.

SCHEDULE: Grounds open daily. Closed Christmas and New Year's Day. Four park buildings open to public: Chatham Manor, Fredericksburg Battlefield Visitor Center, Chancellorsville Battle-field Visitor Center, and Jackson Shrine.

ENTRANCE FEE: none

TOURS: Self-guided auto tour begins at Fredericksburg Battle-field Visitor Center and passes through all 4 battlefields within park. Sixteen tour stops. Walking trails at each battlefield. Visitors can rent or purchase audiotapes to accompany tours.

POINTS OF INTEREST:
  ■ **Fredericksburg National Cemetery** Located near Fredericksburg Visitor Center. ■ **Jackson Shrine** Located on Va. 606. From park take I-95, US 1, or Va. 2.

NEARBY HISTORIC INNS:
  ■ Fredericksburg Colonial Inn (1928), Fredericksburg; (703) 371-5666. ■ Kenmore Inn (1795), Fredericksburg; (703) 371-7622. ■ La Vista Plantation (1838), Fredericksburg; (703) 898-8444. ■ Richard Johnston Inn (1788), Fredericksburg; (703) 899-7606. ■ Selby House Bed & Breakfast (c. 1880), Fredericksburg; (703) 373-7037.

PETERSBURG

Petersburg, Virginia, located 23 miles south of Richmond, possessed enormous strategic importance. Five railroads and nine wagon roads converged on the city, making it one of the Old Dominion's leading transportation hubs. Moreover, all but one railroad serving Richmond from the south funneled first through Petersburg. Thus the fate of the Confederate capital depended upon the security of its neighbor on the Appomattox River.

The armies arrived at Petersburg following five solid weeks of combat across central Virginia. Grant's Overland Campaign commenced in early May 1864 at the Wilderness and met a grievous end on June 3 east of Richmond. His Union troops charged Lee's line of entrenchments near a crossroads tavern named Cold Harbor and lost 7,000 soldiers in several hours. Grant's efforts to maneuver Lee into an open fight had failed.

Grant now adopted a remarkable plan. He would quietly disengage from Lee's army at Cold Harbor, cross the wide James River on a pontoon bridge, and seize Petersburg. In cooperation with the Union Army of the James, Grant would then threaten Richmond from the south, severing the capital's communications with the rest of the Confederacy.

The Union operation began splendidly. On June 15 two Federal corps approached Petersburg from the east, meeting only a handful of Southern soldiers manning a small portion of the city's defense line. Petersburg should have been captured that evening. But timid Union generalship influenced by the disaster at Cold Harbor resulted in only marginal success. The same story recurred during the next two days. Limited Federal attacks gobbled up more of the Confederate line but failed to achieve a breakthrough. On June 18 Lee's army arrived at last from north of the James, ending Grant's best opportunity to reduce Petersburg.

Both armies now constructed elaborate field fortifications while Grant implemented a patient scheme to take the city. The Northerners concentrated on cutting Petersburg's supply routes, particularly the Weldon Railroad leading south and the Southside Railroad running west. Lee stretched his army ever thinner

CAMPAIGN FACTS
Richmond

Campaign dates	May 4, 1864–April 2, 1865
Combat strength	U.S. 134,000; C.S. 89,000
Casualties	U.S. 15,000; C.S. 5,000
Commanders	U.S. Lt. Gen. Ulysses S. Grant Maj. Gen. George G. Meade (Army of the Potomac) C.S. Gen. Robert E. Lee

to neutralize Grant's relentless pressure until eventually he defended more than 60 miles of trenches from east of Richmond to southwest of Petersburg.

One spectacular episode interrupted the routine. On July 30 a regiment of Pennsylvania coal miners exploded a mine beneath a Confederate strongpoint. The blast carved a crater 170 feet long, 60 feet wide, and 30 feet deep. Grant considered the assault that followed "the saddest affair I have witnessed in the war." Thousands of leaderless soldiers plunged into the crater rather than going around it and became helpless

CAMPAIGN FACTS
Petersburg

Campaign dates	June 15, 1864–April 2, 1865
Combat strength	U.S. 109,000; C.S. 59,000
Casualties	U.S. 42,000; C.S. 28,000
Commanders	U.S. Lt. Gen. Ulysses S. Grant Maj. Gen. George G. Meade (Army of the Potomac) Maj. Gen. Benjamin F. Butler Maj. Gen. E. O. C. Ord (Army of the James) C.S. Gen. Robert E. Lee

targets for a Confederate counter-attack. The bungled offensive cost Grant 4,000 men.

The Federals resumed their slow strangulation in August, breaking the Weldon Railroad on the 18th. The next month, Grant's simultaneous initiatives on both sides of the James extended Union lines three miles west of the tracks and

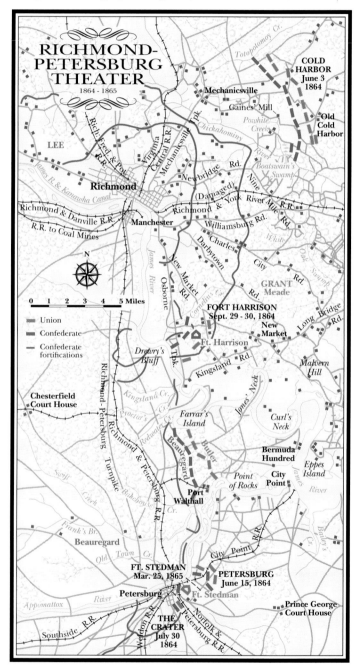

RICHMOND-PETERSBURG THEATER
1864 - 1865

COLD HARBOR
June 3 1864

Old Cold Harbor

Mechanicsville

Gaines' Mill

LEE

Rich. Fred. & Pot. R.R.

Virginia Central R.R.

Mechanicsville Tpk.

Chickahominy River

Powhite Creek

Boatswain's Swamp

James R. & Kanawha Canal

Richmond

Newbridge Rd.

(Damaged)

Nine Mile Rd.

Richmond & York River R.R.

Richmond & Danville R.R.

R.R. to Coal Mines

Manchester

Williamsburg Rd.

Charles City Rd.

Darbytown

White Oak Swamp

N

James River

New Market Rd.

Osborne

Coggins Cr.

GRANT
Meade

Long Bridge Rd.

0 1 2 3 4 5 Miles

Union
Confederate
Confederate fortifications

FORT HARRISON
Sept. 29 - 30, 1864
New Market

Ft. Harrison

Drewry's Bluff

Kingsland Rd.

Malvern Hill

Chesterfield Court House

Kingsland Cr.

Richmond & Petersburg Turnpike

Proctor's Cr.

Redwater Cr.

Farrar's Island

Jones' Neck

Curl's Neck

Beauregard

Butler

Bermuda Hundred

Eppes Island

Richmond & Petersburg R.R.

Point of Rocks

City Point

James River

Swift Cr.

Bailey's Cr.

Port Walthall

Frank's Br.

Beauregard

Old Town Cr.

City Point R.R.

FT. STEDMAN
Mar. 25, 1865

PETERSBURG
June 15, 1864

Petersburg

Appomattox River

Southside R.R.

Weldon R.R.

Ft. Stedman

THE CRATER
July 30 1864

Norfolk & Petersburg R.R.

Prince George Court House

overran Newmarket Heights and Fort Harrison southeast of Richmond. Winter weather ended active operations, but Lee's devoted army now struggled with miserable conditions in the frozen trenches, subsisting on starvation rations. Although the Federals also suffered, their huge supply base at City Point, connected to the front by a military railroad, provided all the food and equipment they needed.

Desperate times called for desperate action. With the coming of spring Lee authorized an attack against Fort Stedman, an earthen bastion east of Petersburg only 150 yards from the Confederate lines. He hoped that by carrying the fort and penetrating Grant's front, he would force the Federals to con-strict their lines to the west, open-ing an escape route for his army. The attack on March 25, 1865, succeeded initially, but Union counterthrusts repaired the damage, inflicting 4,000 casualties on Lee's demoralized army.

Now Lee's only hope was to gather supplies and dash west before Grant irretrievably tight-ened the Petersburg noose. On April 1 at Five Forks, an intersec-tion 17 miles southwest of Peters-burg, Union forces under Maj. Gen. Philip Sheridan drove 10,000 Confederates away from the Southside Railroad, sealing the last supply route into the city. Lee mounted a heroic defense on April 2 against Grant's general assault and advised President Jefferson Davis to evacuate Richmond. That night Lee's ragged survivors filed out of Petersburg hoping to rendezvous with Richmond's retreating defenders and make their way to North Carolina. Appomattox was but a week away.

PARK INFORMATION

HEADQUARTERS: Petersburg National Battlefield, P. O. Box 549, Petersburg, VA 23804. Telephone: (804) 732-3531.

DIRECTIONS: Located in Petersburg, 25 miles south of Richmond on I-95. Visitor Center is off Va. 36, just east of Petersburg.

SCHEDULE: Park grounds open daily from 8 a.m. until dusk. Visitor Center open daily from 8 a.m. to 5 p.m. and from mid-June to mid-August until 7 p.m. Closed Christmas and New Year's Day.

ENTRANCE FEE: $3.00 per car, $1.00 per bus passenger. Disabled and age 62 or older admitted free.

TOURS: During summer, 20-minute walking tours beginning at Visitor Center offered 4 times daily. Four-mile, self-guided auto tour offers wayside exhibits and audio stations at 8 tour stops. Longer, 16-mile tour follows siege and defense lines.

POINTS OF INTEREST: ■ **Petersburg Visitor Center** Features bookstore and 17-minute map presentation. ■ **City Point Visitor Contact Station** Located in Appomattox Manor. Two rooms in antebellum house furnished with period antiques. ■ **Five Forks Visitor Contact Station** Open during summer months. Ranger on duty.

NEARBY HISTORIC INNS: ■ Edgewood Plantation (c. 1849), Charles City; (804) 829-2962. ■ North Bend Plantation Bed & Breakfast (1819), Charles City; (804) 829-5176. ■ Piney Grove at Southall's Plantation (c. 1800), Charles City; (804) 829-2480.

APPOMATTOX COURT HOUSE

The village of Appomattox Court House, a tiny collection of buildings that served as the seat of Appomattox County, Virginia, slumbered far from the path of Civil War armies. In fact, the hamlet's isolation is what attracted Wilmer McLean. McLean's plantation near Manassas received substantial damage during the war's first major battle, so he sought a retreat far from the cannon's roar to sit out the hostilities. In one of history's small ironies, McLean's Appomattox home hosted the symbolic end to the conflict from which he had fled.

The armies reached Appomattox after a week-long campaign commencing in Petersburg. Lee and his Army of Northern Virginia left that doomed city on the night of April 2, 1865, hoping to rendezvous with Richmond's retreating defenders at Amelia Court House

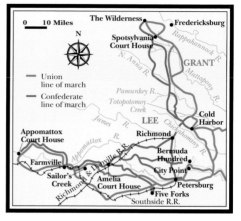

▼ *McLean House, Appomattox*

40 miles to the west. The combined Confederate forces expected supply trains to meet them at Amelia. With his men properly fed and equipped, Lee planned to march southwest to unite with Gen. Joseph E. Johnston's troops in North Carolina.

Much to Lee's disappointment, the anticipated rations did not reach Amelia. Now his soldiers had to push ahead, foraging the countryside while Grant's Federal armies doggedly pursued them. Grant aimed to prevent the Confederates from turning south. In a running battle that included the capture of

more than 7,000 Southerners on April 6 at Sailor's Creek, Grant placed troops astride each of Lee's potential escape routes near Appomattox Court House. "There is nothing left for me to do but to go and see General Grant," admitted Lee, "and I would rather die a thousand deaths."

The generals met in McLean's parlor on the afternoon of April 9. Following an awkward conversation about their service together in the Mexican War, Lee and Grant addressed the business at hand. The surrender terms were simple. Lee's soldiers would be paroled and sent home. As paroled prisoners, they pledged not to fight again until they had been formally exchanged for the Union soldiers still in Confederate prisons—a purely technical point, since the Southern war effort was all but over. Grant permitted the Rebels to take their horses with them to assist in planting the spring crop, a gesture Lee thought would "have the best possible effect upon the men." The documents signed, Lee stepped out on McLean's porch, smote his fist into his palm several times, and rode off to break the sad news to the remnant of his proud command.

The surrender ceremonies concluded on April 12, exactly four years after the first firing on Fort Sumter. Some 28,000 Confederates laid down their arms, General Lee's parting order soothing their hearts: "With an unceasing admiration of your constancy and devotion to your Country and a grateful remembrance of your kind and generous consideration for myself, I bid you all an affectionate farewell."

WEST VIRGINIA

T he secession crisis aggra-
vated deep animosities
between the older counties
of eastern Virginia and newer ones
in the mountains and valleys west
of the Alleghenies. Many western
Virginians believed that politicians
in Richmond ignored them, and
when Virginia seceded, western
leaders called for the creation of
a new state. Virginians in the
northwest applauded victories by
Maj. Gen. George B. McClellan's
Union forces at Philippi on June 3,
Rich Mountain on July 11, and
Carrick's Ford on July 13 (Confederate Brig. Gen. Robert S. Garnett,
the first Civil War general to die
in combat, was killed at Carrick's
Ford).

While the armies maneuvered,
representatives from western counties attended two conventions in
Wheeling. Delegates at the first,
held in mid-May, opted not to
secede from Virginia. The second
convention, which convened on
June 11, declared secession from
the Union unconstitutional and
pronounced itself the true government of Virginia. Fueled by
separationists in counties bordering
Pennsylvania and Maryland, plan-
ning went forward in Wheeling
to form a 48-county state called
Kanawha. Although many of
these counties were not represented at Wheeling and harbored
Confederate majorities, an October referendum in which only
Unionists were allowed to vote
endorsed the idea.

A constitutional convention met in Wheeling between November 1861 and February 1862. The delegates framed a constitution and dropped the name Kanawha in favor of West Virginia, which now encompassed 50 counties. Jefferson and Berkeley counties, through which ran the Baltimore & Ohio Railroad, had been brought in despite secessionist majorities to secure that vital rail link for the North. Voters in the designated counties ratified the constitution on April 3, 1862, in an election boycotted by pro-Confederates; the Unionist government in Wheeling added its approval on May 13. After subsequent negotiations with Lincoln and Congress yielded an agreement to abolish slavery in the new state, West Virginia became the 35th member of the Union on June 20, 1863.

An artificial creation in many respects, West Virginia remained divided throughout the war. From a white population of 355,526 in 1860 came 31,872 Union soldiers and roughly 15,000 Confederates. Fewer than 200 of the region's 18,371 enslaved and 2,791 free blacks served in Federal units. Union dead totaled 4,017, while Confederate losses are unknown. Four Confederate generals, including Thomas J. "Stonewall" Jackson, were born in the counties of West Virginia, as were Jesse Lee Reno and three other Union generals.

Small-scale campaigns, cavalry raids, and guerrilla operations characterized military activity in West Virginia. Following McClellan's early victories, Robert E. Lee conducted his unsuccessful Cheat Mountain campaign of September 10–15, 1861. Union troops based in West Virginia fought against Stonewall Jackson during the 1862 Shenandoah Valley Campaign, and Confederates under Maj. Gen. William W. Loring captured and held Charleston briefly in September 1862. Brig. Gens. William E. Jones and John D. Imboden led Confederate cavalry against the B & O Railroad and threatened Wheeling in the spring of 1863. Overall, the state suffered relatively moderate damage during the war, though bitter feelings from the conflict endured for many years.

◀ *Harpers Ferry from Maryland Heights*

HARPERS FERRY

Thomas Jefferson declared in his *Notes on the State of Virginia* that the geographic splendor of Harpers Ferry, where the Shenandoah and Potomac Rivers join and flow east through a cleft in the Blue Ridge, "is worth a voyage across the Atlantic." In the 19th century, a vibrant industrial village, absorbed in the manufacture of firearms, added the bustle of workshops and railroads to the scene. But by 1865 Harpers Ferry lay in ruins, a victim of the Civil War.

Events in Harpers Ferry helped precipitate the conflict that caused its demise. A fanatical abolitionist named John Brown, who earned a reputation as a violent antislavery leader in "Bleeding Kansas," targeted Harpers Ferry as the site for a revolution. After three years of secret fund-raising and preparation, Brown led a band of 21 men into Harpers Ferry on the night of October 16, 1859. He hoped to incite a slave rebellion, arm the insurgents with weapons from the arsenal, and conduct a guerrilla war of liberation from the surrounding mountains.

The outcome of the raid reflected its flaws. No slaves joined Brown's "army," and when the local militia rallied to resist his half-baked scheme, Brown could think of nothing better than to seek refuge in the armory firehouse. Lt. Col. Robert E. Lee and Lt. J. E. B. Stuart soon arrived in Harpers Ferry at the head of a contingent of U.S. Marines from Washington, who stormed Brown's fort on the morning of October 18 and put an end to the episode.

Brown stood trial for treason, murder, and conspiring to cause insurrection, and judge and jury condemned him to death. Moments before his execution on December 2, Brown handed his jailor a note: "I John Brown am now quite certain that the crimes of this guilty, land will never be purged away; but with Blood."

Brown's prophecy came true 16 months later, in part because of his quixotic raid. Southerners considered Brown a madman and dangerous criminal, pointing to the statutes to justify their views. Many Northerners praised Brown's devotion to a higher law, and his death on the gallows martyred him. The South noted this reaction with alarm, and the breach between the sections widened.

In Virginia that gulf grew unbridgeable after the events at Fort Sumter. On April 17, 1861, the Old Dominion left the Union. The ink had not dried on Virginia's ordinance of secession when a makeshift Rebel army descended on Harpers Ferry. A token guard of 45 U.S. soldiers set the arsenal ablaze and attempted to destroy the shops and equipment as well. Some 15,000 rifles went up in flames, but the Confederates removed most of the weapons-making supplies, providing the nucleus for Southern arms manufacturing early in the war.

Within a week about 1,300 motley Virginia volunteers had gathered at Harpers Ferry. Col. Thomas J. Jackson of the Virginia Military Institute assumed command and soon, marveled one officer, "Perfect order reigned everywhere." In addition, Jackson managed to capture a large number of trains, complete with badly needed locomotives, by cleverly manipulating credulous Northern railroad officials. When Brig. Gen. Joseph E. Johnston arrived in May to take charge in the name of the Confederate States, he inherited a well-ordered and efficient military operation.

Johnston and Jackson withdrew from Harpers Ferry in June and a month later participated in the Confederate victory at First Manassas. Union troops then occupied the town, which next entered the strategic picture in September 1862. Lee, now a Confederate general in command of the Army of Northern Virginia, had crossed the Potomac River downstream from Harpers Ferry intent on raiding into Pennsylvania. His intended supply line ran down the Shenandoah Valley and across the Potomac near Harpers Ferry, which was held by a Union garrison. Lee needed to eliminate the Federals at Harpers Ferry in order to sustain his offensive.

Ironically, the Union field commander, Maj. Gen. George B. McClellan, requested that Harpers Ferry be evacuated and its troops added to his Army of the Potomac, now slowly pursuing Lee in Maryland. But officials in Washington refused to abandon the town,

counting on McClellan to relieve the vulnerable garrison.

To capture Harpers Ferry, Lee boldly divided his army on September 10. He sent Jackson at the head of three divisions on a wide sweep from the west. Two divisions under Maj. Gen. Lafayette McLaws approached Elk Ridge and moved south toward Maryland Heights, overlooking Harpers Ferry from the north bank of the Potomac. Another wing led by Brig. Gen. John G. Walker crossed the Potomac and climbed Loudoun Heights on the southeast bank of the Shenandoah opposite the town.

Joined by troops fleeing Jackson's approach, Union forces in Harpers Ferry numbered almost 14,000. Their commander, Col. Dixon S. Miles, posted a brigade on Maryland Heights and other units west of town on high ground called Bolivar Heights, hoping to hold fast until McClellan appeared.

On September 13 some of McLaws's men drove away the defenders on Maryland Heights, whose unauthorized retreat from the dominating terrain all but doomed Miles's position. Walker placed artillery on undefended Loudoun Heights, and Jackson

⤸⤸ BATTLE FACTS ⤸⤸

Battle dates	September 13–15, 1862
Combat strength	U.S. 14,000; C.S. 24,000
Casualties	U.S. 12,700 (12,500 captured); C.S. 286
Commanders	U.S. Col. Dixon S. Miles C.S. Maj. Gen. Thomas J. Jackson

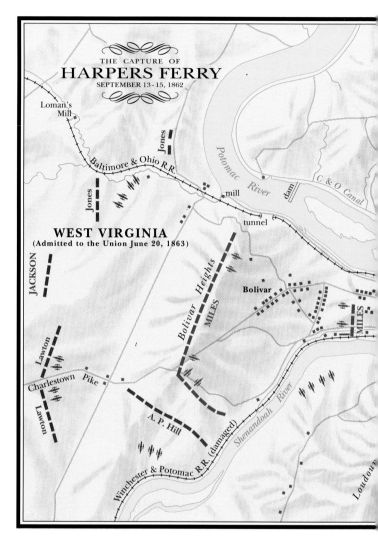

THE CAPTURE OF
HARPERS FERRY
SEPTEMBER 13-15, 1862

Loman's Mill

Baltimore & Ohio R.R.

Jones

Jones

Potomac River

C & O Canal

mill

dam

tunnel

WEST VIRGINIA
(Admitted to the Union June 20, 1863)

JACKSON

Bolivar Heights

MILES

Bolivar

MILES

Lawton

Charlestown Pike

Lawton

A. P. Hill

Shenandoah River

Winchester & Potomac R.R. (damaged)

Loudoun

arrived on School House Ridge facing the Union line west of town. The next day a part of McClellan's army scattered McLaws's rear guard at Crampton's Gap on South Mountain, but the local Federal commander thought his force too small to exploit his advantage. His refusal to attack Maryland Heights ended Miles's last hope for redemption.

That night, while 1,400 blueclad cavalry executed a daring escape across the Potomac, Jackson maneuvered one of his divisions behind Miles's left flank on Bolivar Heights. The presence of this infantry and a devastating artillery bombardment from three directions convinced Miles to surrender on the morning of the 15th. A stray shell exploded near the unlucky colonel, inflicting a mortal wound, so Miles's second-in-command conducted the formal capitulation. Jackson's rewards included 12,500 prisoners, 13,000 small arms, and 73 cannon. "Boys,

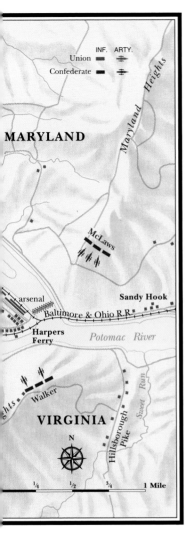

MARYLAND

Maryland Heights

INF.   ARTY.
Union ▬ ≣
Confederate ▬ ≣

McLaws

arsenal
Baltimore & Ohio R.R.

Sandy Hook

Harpers
Ferry

Potomac   River

Walker

Heights

VIRGINIA

Hillsborough Pike

Sweet Run

N

¼   ½   ¾   1 Mile

he's not much for looks," admitted a Northern private gazing at the legendary Stonewall, "but if we'd had him we wouldn't have been caught in this trap!"

Harpers Ferry continued to play an important role throughout the war, serving as the fortified supply base for Maj. Gen. Philip Sheridan's successful Shenandoah Valley Campaign in 1864. Sheridan's elimination of Confederate threats in the Valley at last removed Harpers Ferry from danger.

A. WILSON GREENE, a native Chicagoan, earned degrees in history from Florida State University and Louisiana State University. Greene served as a historian and manager with the National Park Service for 16 years and is now the executive director of the Association for the Preservation of Civil War Sites, based in Fredericksburg, Virginia. He has written several books on the Civil War, the latest entitled *Whatever You Resolve to Be: Essays on Stonewall Jackson*; his articles and essays on the period have appeared in many publications.

GARY W. GALLAGHER heads the Department of History at Pennsylvania State University. Born in California and raised in Colorado, he received a B.A. from Adams State College and an M.A. and Ph.D. from the University of Texas at Austin. Gallagher is the author or editor of six books on the Civil War, including *Stephen Dodson Ramseur: Lee's Gallant General* and *The First Day at Gettysburg: Essays on Confederate and Union Leadership*. A longtime advocate of efforts to protect Civil War sites, Gallagher has been president of the Association for the Preservation of Civil War Sites since its founding in 1987.

SAM ABELL, born and reared in Sylvania, Ohio, has been contributing images to National Geographic publications since 1970. His magazine stories include "The Wonderland of Lewis Carroll," "The World of Tolstoy," "The Shakers' Brief Eternity," and "Journey into Dreamtime," a vision of northwestern Australia. Among his Geographic books are *Still Waters, White Waters: Exploring America's Rivers and Lakes* and *The Pacific Crest Trail*. In addition to his Society work, Abell has published five books, including two on the Civil War. In 1990, Abell's work was collected in a mid-career retrospective entitled *Stay This Moment*, which comprised a book and exhibition at New York's International Center of Photography.

LIVING HISTORY PRESENTATIONS

The following parks offer living history presentations: Antietam, Md.; Chickamauga and Chattanooga, Ga. and Tenn.; Fort Donelson, Tenn.; Fort Pulaski, Ga.; Fort Sumter, S.C.; Fredericksburg and Spotsylvania, Va.; Gettysburg, Pa.; Harpers Ferry, W.Va.; Kennesaw Mountain, Ga.; Manassas, Va.; Monocacy, Md.; Pea Ridge, Ark.; Petersburg, Va.; Richmond, Va.; Stones River, Tenn.; Vicksburg, Miss.; and Wilson's Creek, Mo. Contact the park headquarters for schedules of events.